Divorce
and **Separation**

A practical guide to making smart decisions

Two years ago Fiona McAuslan asked me to write a promotional review of Living With Separation and Divorce written with her co-author, Peter Nicholson. I read their book and readily agreed to provide an endorsement. I was impressed with the quality and clarity of the information provided, the conversational and welcoming tone and the effective use of illustrations to complement the well-written text. Having been a family mediator for over 30 years, and divorce attorney prior to that, I was familiar with the popular and professional literature on the legal and emotional concerns of divorcing couples, on how to manage post-divorce parenting and on financial matters related to divorce. Living With Separation and Divorce fills a void in the divorce literature. It is unique. It is neither an instruction manual nor a list of pre-packaged options for dealing with finances and parenting. Instead, the book is a practical guide that helps divorcing couples work together—to discuss and find workable solutions to matters of parenting and finances. The underlying premise is that divorcing couples are best positioned to understand their family's needs and to make smart decisions.

In addition to writing a review, I flew to Dublin to attend the book launch. While there, I asked Fiona and Peter whether they were interested in collaborating on a version of their book for a US audience. The result is this book; one that retains the basic premise and goals of the original while updating information for a US reader.

Michael Lang, family mediator, professor of Conflict Resolution and former editor-in-chief of Mediation Quarterly, Sarasota, Florida

Divorce
and Separation

California Edition

A practical guide to making smart decisions

TESTIMONIALS

A Google search for 'self-help divorce books' will return several hundred choices, so why this one? Simple, in all my years of dealing with every nuanced issue and aspect couples go through and experience in the process of separating, divorcing and, when children are involved, building a post-divorce family, this one does it all. From the legal procedural steps, to methodologies (i.e., mediation to litigation), to the inevitable psychological and emotional stages everyone goes through, it's here. Frankly, if every couple contemplating separating and divorcing took the time to read this book, this all-to-frequent life occurrence would be far less disruptive and they'd be better equipped for the next stage in their lives.

> Mark Ressa, Certified Family Law Specialist
> and Past Chair wto the Family Law Section of the California State Bar

I love this book. It not only empowers the reader, it provides as close to a roadmap for divorce and separation as you can get. Dissolution is a scary, daunting process but this guide breaks it down into bite-sized pieces making it all more manageable. I highly recommend Divorce and Separation for anyone going through a marital split.

> Susan Pease Gadoua, LCSW and author of
> the San Francisco Chronicle bestseller, Contemplating Divorce

This is not only a fabulous, immensely useful, easy-to-read, user-friendly book on divorce and separation, it is the only one I have come across in over 38 years of practice that is both legally accurate and emotionally intelligent. It offers practical advice, concrete steps, well-considered alternatives and real-life stories of parents and kids who have gone through the process, plus an incredible list of websites that is easily worth much more than the price. This book will make the process far less damaging, conflicted and confusing than it otherwise is.

> Kenneth Cloke, author of The Dance of Opposites:
> Explorations in Mediation, Dialogue and Conflict Resolution Systems Design

Divorce can feel overwhelming – there is so much to learn. Divorce and Separation provides you with practical information in easy to understand language: financial and asset check lists, ideas for parenting plans, sample agreements, helpful links, and definitions of legal terms all in one book. More importantly, the authors provide suggestions for productive conversations with your spouse, tips on creating a supportive environment for your children, how to choose and customize the best process (negotiation, mediation, litigation) that works for you, and supportive advice in working through emotional issues as you transition to a new chapter of your life.

> Nina Meierding, Former President of the Academy of Family Mediators

Divorce and Separation walks readers through an often overwhelming emotional and financial event in straightforward, concise and easy-to-understand language. It's a valuable guide for anyone considering or undergoing a marital breakup, and the personal experiences will help readers feel less alone and scared about what's ahead.

> Vicki Larson, award-winning journalist, blogger and co-author of
> The New I Do: Reshaping Marriage for Skeptics, Realists and Rebels

CONTENTS

INTRODUCTION

When couples separate they face emotional upheaval. They also need to make important decisions affecting everyone around them, especially their children.

Divorce and Separation is the one book about divorce that starts with the premise: This is your life. These are your decisions. You are the ones who really understand your family. You are capable of making wise, responsible choices. So, here are some methods to help you talk about and make smart decisions.

Divorce and Separation is a simple guide to mutual problem solving. It will NOT tell you what to do. It will NOT make judgments about how you have lived your life, or how you should live in the future. It will NOT give you legal or financial advice.

What this book WILL DO is help you figure out what you need to discuss. It WILL help you gather information to help you make wise choices for you and your family. It WILL point to a number of helpful options. And, it WILL help you decide what is what is best for you and your family.

There is no road map to a successful divorce—don't let anyone tell you otherwise. Your family is unique, your needs are unique, and the solutions must be unique. We wrote this book to show couples how to take control of the decisions they are facing.

The first step is to realize that the confusion and anxiety you are experiencing are real and universally experienced by couples who are considering or have decided to separate and divorce. The breakdown of a relationship is hard. Your life will change. The person you are parting from was once the person you thought you would be with for the rest of your life. The dreams, plans and expectations you had for your family are ending.

Divorce and Separation will help you think about difficult decisions:

• what each of you will do to care for your children and look out for them

• how you will manage as parents living in two households

• the best ways for you to use the family income in order to provide for two households

• how you want to divide your assets (what you own) and debts (what you owe)

• when and how you will tell the children and how to deal with their questions

• what to do about your family and friends who are concerned about you, your children and your spouse

• and, most importantly, how you will talk with one another about the divorce so that you can make all these decisions together.

We believe this book, like your family, is unique. You can find books that talk about how to manage post-divorce parenting or coping with the emotional impact of divorce.

Divorce and Separation contains specific information about and resources for divorce in California. It is a guide to help you work together to create fair, workable and practical decisions for you and your family.

Divorce and Separation is not pop-psychology; it does not offer pre-packaged answers. It does not offer one-size-fits-all financial solutions. And, it won't tell you how to fight and win.

Divorce and Separation will help you work together through "mutual problem solving." Using this method, even highly conflicted couples can develop smart decisions about separation, children and finances. We help you and your spouse create these solutions through activities, guided lessons and presentation of helpful information.

The book is a guide to help you address key issues such as whether and when to separate, how to make smart choices and ways to structure your finances to provide for the family's needs.

children   manage their divorce

emotional upheaval

mutual problem solving

confusion and anxiety   divorce

good choices

gather information   finances

separation   change

choices

If there is one single message we want you to take from **Divorce and Separation** it is that you are in charge of the decisions. The choices are yours and no one else's. No one knows your family as well as you do, so no one can tell you what you should do. You can ask questions. You can get advice. In the end, the decisions are yours to make.

smart decisions

family

breakdown of a relationship

two households

financial questions

assets and debts

workable decisions

difficult decisions

income and expenses

Visit us online for information on other support agencies in California.

We have researched and generated a comprehensive list of additional resources, government bodies and support agencies that can advise you on your divorce or separation.

This resource is continuously updated so do check it from time to time for updates.

The website also has a number of other helpful downloads including:
- Budget sheets
- Parenting plans
- Sample Marital Settlement Agreement
- Income and Expense Declaration and Schedule of Assets and Debts
- Helpful tips for determining child support

You can also see the views of and interviews with other professionals in the fields of mediation, law, finance and children, as well as other useful information and tips.

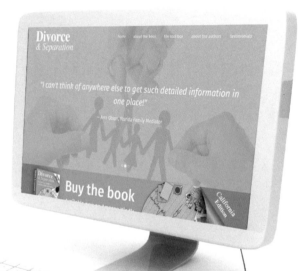

www.DivorceBookCalifornia.com

ABOUT THE AUTHORS

Michael Lang For more than 40 years, as a practitioner, educator, author and advocate for mediation, Michael has been a leading voice in the field of separation, divorce and mediation. As a family mediator, Michael has assisted hundreds of separating and divorcing couples. As a trainer he has designed and presented mediation and conflict management courses and workshops in court systems, government agencies, not-for-profit organizations and university faculties. As an educator Michael created one of the first graduate programs in conflict resolution in the US. He has been a visiting faculty member at a number of law schools and graduate programs and has been a featured speaker at professional meetings throughout the U.S. and Canada as well as in Ireland, the UK, Australia and Trinidad. Michael is the co-author of The Making of a Mediator: Developing Artistry in Practice.

Fiona A. McAuslan holds a Master's in Mediation and Conflict Resolution Studies from University College Dublin. She is an experienced mediator and conflict coach with many years' experience working with family, workplace and school conflicts. She works in the Irish Family Mediation Service and Clanwilliam Institute and is an accredited practitioner mediator with the Mediators' Institute of Ireland. Fiona has published The S.A.L.T. Programme: A Conflict Resolution Education Programme for Primary Schools. She lives in North County Dublin with her husband Michael, and her children Sarah and Ben.

Peter Nicholson is a communications specialist and has built a very successful marketing and visual communications business over the last fifteen years. Peter and Fiona met while working on the S.A.L.T. programme and they have continued to work together on many other projects. He is married to Karen, and they have two children, Patrick and Ailish.

Over the last number of years, Fiona and Peter have published a number of self-help books for children in the Resolving Books series. These books cover many subjects such as bullying, anger, sibling rivalry, bereavement and separation. For more information on the Resolving Books, visit www.resolvingbooks.com. The illustrations in this book are by Kelly Sheridan, who has worked with Fiona and Peter on a number of other projects in the past.

Mark B. Baer attended law school because of his personal experiences as a child of his parents' very contentious litigated divorce and what he saw as the misuse of the legal system by people seeking emotional justice. As a result of those experiences, when he started practicing law over twenty-five years ago, he steered away from heavily emotional areas of law. Ironically, a few years later, he found himself practicing in the field of family law, a field he had deliberately avoided because he didn't want to assist parents in unintentionally harming their children by escalating the level of parental conflict by fighting against each other. For a while, he believed that he could practice within the adversarial system and help children by doing so in a psychologically-minded and child-centered manner in spite of the approach taken by the opposing side. Once he realized otherwise, he learned about mediation, received extensive mediation training, focused his practice on mediation and began publishing prolifically on the interplay between psychology and conflict resolution within the field of family law, as well as familial and interpersonal relationships in general. His articles have been referenced in books, law review articles, and by non-political evidenced-based public policy think tanks.

At the end of the day, the decisions are yours. You started a relationship together and now you have to consider how to work together to end the relationship. As the two people who started a relationship together you now have to deal with the many decisions that come about because of the end of that relationship. **Divorce and Separation** will provide helpful information and general advice. It will help you focus on what you each need to do to achieve a positive future after your separation or divorce. What it will not do is tell you what you should do; that's up to you.

A couple of notes about the language in this book.

(1) We use the word "spouse" or "partner" to mean any life partner. We have written this book to help married and unmarried couples. While California has laws that specifically relate to married couples, the information in this book should be helpful to anyone in a committed relationship, or who are parents of minor children.

(2) We use the term "marriage" to mean any loving and significant relationship, not only one that has been sanctioned under law.

(3) We use the term "divorce" or the term "separation" to mean the ending of a relationship. Even couples who are married sometimes may choose to separate without going through a legal divorce.

As you start reading this book, you may be
feeling overwhelmed by all you face
and all the advice you are getting.

At the end of the day, two people who started a relationship together now have to deal with the end of that relationship.

This book will help you focus on what you each need to do to achieve a positive future after your separation.

4 METHODS FOR COMPLETING YOUR DIVORCE

When you think about your separation and divorce, there is so much that you need to consider. Your life will be different. Just thinking about those changes can seem overwhelming. And then, there are all the decisions you need to make—among the most important are: whether you will co-parent and how; calculating child support and whether there will be spousal support; figuring out how to divide your assets and debts. Coping with the changes and making these decisions can at times seem impossible. That's understandable. Use this book to help you figure out what you need to decide, pull together the information you'll need, and decide how you want to make decisions—together or with help from a professional.

One of the first things to consider is how you and your spouse want to talk about and deal with all the decisions you face. We will describe four basic methods, negotiation (we call this sitting at the kitchen table), mediation, collaborative law, and litigation (going to court).

Before we talk about these methods, there are two pieces of advice we want to share—the only advice we offer in this book.

1. This is your life. You know best what's right for you and for your family. Remember this when family and friends try to be helpful. You may hear: "let me tell you what I got in my divorce," or "you should fight for custody" or "get a good lawyer and take her/him to court." They all mean well; they all want to help. Ultimately you are in the best position to know what's right.

2. Sometimes you may want or need professional advice such as from a lawyer, counselor or financial consultant. We encourage you to listen to the advice, ask good questions, and then do only what you think is best for you and your family.

What follows are descriptions and flow charts for the four most commonly used methods for completing your divorce. Each one has its advantages and its disadvantages. Each of these approaches works. Each one will help you get through your divorce. There is no one right way to do this. The right method is the one that is best for you. As with every other topic in this book, we don't tell you what you should do. Our goal is to provide helpful, practical information so you can decide for yourself what's right.

Here is some information about the four methods that may help you decide how to proceed.

Kitchen Table Negotiation:
This method might work for you if you and your spouse can talk with each other and if together you made good decisions in the past. Benefits include: it is personal; it is faster and less expensive; you schedule time to talk when it suits you; and everything is private. On the other hand, these conversations can be intense and sometimes emotionally difficult; they are difficult if you have a history of not being able to make decisions together; and they are not advisable if there has been any domestic abuse.

Mediation:
Mediation involves a person who helps you talk constructively together, understands the issues that need to be resolved, works with you to come up with a workable agreement, and who does not make decisions for you. Benefits include, it is private and confidential, can be scheduled at your convenience, has a proven track record and you stay in control of all decisions. To use mediation effectively, you'll need to find the right mediator, be willing to pay a professional fee (some no-cost mediation may be available), and as with Kitchen Table Negotiations, you will need to work together with your spouse.

Collaborative Law:
Each spouse hires an attorney trained as a collaborative lawyer. The couple and their attorneys, often with a mental health professional and/or financial professional, meet one or more times. Everyone involved agrees to share information freely and to commit themselves to working cooperatively to find practical and workable solutions. The benefits are generally the same as in mediation, including your ability to make decisions that affect you and your family. Another benefit is the participation of other professionals to offer advice and guidance about parenting and finances.

Court:
Most people have some idea of what lawyers do and what happens in a courtroom. The advantages of going to court are that you have someone speaking for you (your lawyer) and an independent person (judge) listens to the facts and the legal arguments, weighs the evidence and the law, and makes decisions that are binding on you and your spouse. If you decide to take your case to court, you are not in control—you live with what the judge decides; you don't deal directly with your spouse; the conflict between you and your spouse often becomes more heated; usually there are long delays before you can get a court date; and the legal fees can be substantial.

KITCHEN TABLE NEGOTIATION

So, how do you negotiate successfully with your spouse? State your own needs, interests, values and goals. Listen to what matters to your spouse. Communicate effectively. Focus on solving the problem. Be realistic and practical: make the agreement work.

You and your spouse communicate—in person or by phone, text or email—and discuss all the issues and topics you need to resolve. You communicate as often as needed, and in the end come up with a set of agreements that you can live with. These agreements become part of the Judgment for Dissolution of Marriage issued by the Court.

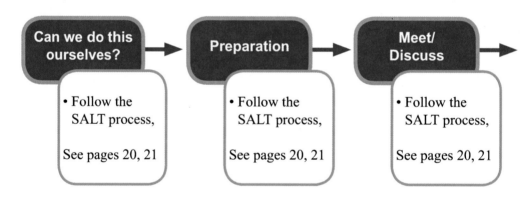

Can we do this ourselves?	Preparation	Meet/ Discuss
• Follow the SALT process, See pages 20, 21	• Follow the SALT process, See pages 20, 21	• Follow the SALT process, See pages 20, 21

Conflict

- Follow the SALT process,

See pages 20, 21

Agreement

- Decide whether one or both of you want to review the terms of your agreement with an attorney. And, decide whether one or both of you will ask an attorney to prepare a written agreement.

See pages 20, 21

Present to Court

- Either you or your attorney presents your Settlement Agreement to the Court.
- The judge will, if everything is in order, issue a Judgment for Dissolution of Marriage.

See pages 20, 21

MEDIATION

The mediator will help you be sure you have a complete list of topics and issues; will help you collect the information you need to make decisions; and will help you deal with one another when conflicts arise. The mediator helps you communicate more effectively and make smart decisions.

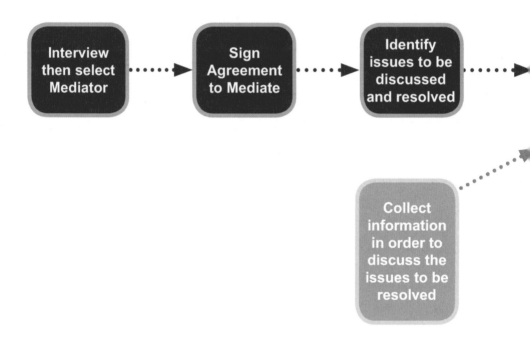

The mediator is impartial and does not make decisions for you (or even give you legal advice). You stay in control of your decisions; the mediator helps you talk with one another, stay on task and work through any disagreements.

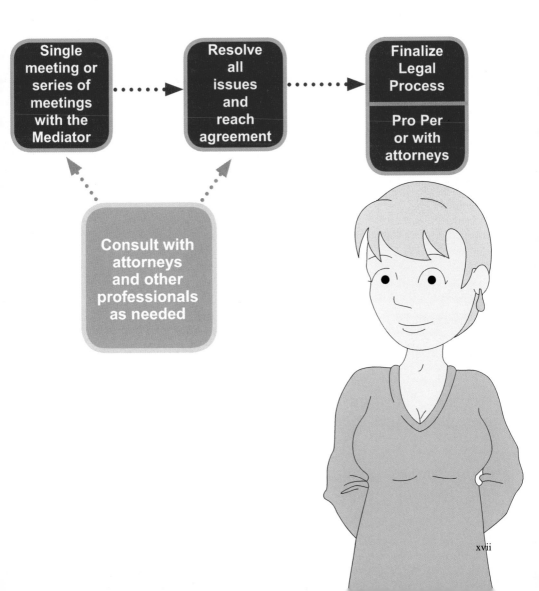

COLLABORATIVE LAW

Each spouse hires an attorney trained as a collaborative lawyer. The couple and their attorneys meet one or more times. The spouses and attorneys sign a participation agreement requiring everyone to share information freely and frankly and committing themselves to work cooperatively to find fair and reasonable solutions. With this method, you may also seek the advice of other professionals, such as financial professionals, to help you make decisions.

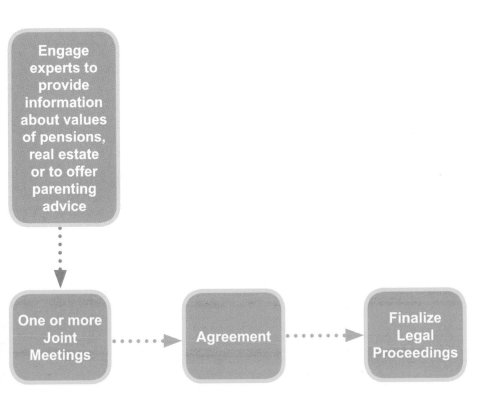

LITIGATION - COURT

Each party presents evidence—testimony and documents—and has the opportunity through their lawyers to challenge (cross-examine) the evidence presented. Lawyers also present arguments to support your position. After considering the evidence, legal rules, and comments from the lawyers, the judge makes a final decision. The judge's decision is then binding on you and your spouse.

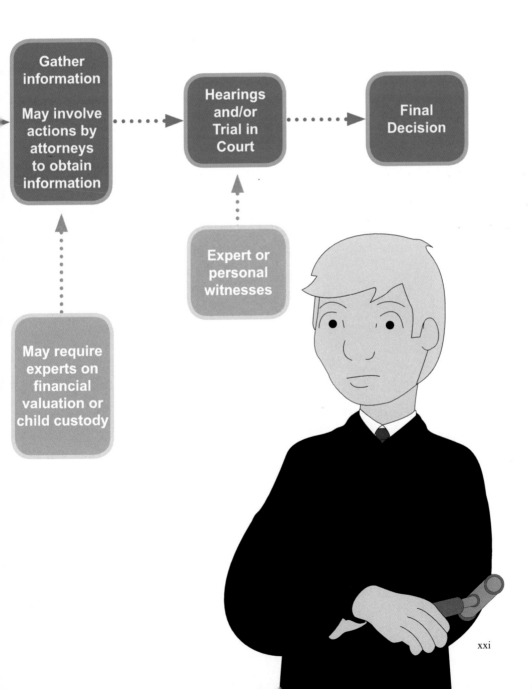

(1)

SEPARATING

The breakdown of a loving relationship is a hard and painful experience. The person you are parting from was once the person you thought you would be with for the rest of your life. As the relationship disintegrates, it can mean the end of the dreams and expectations you both had for the future. And, you are forced to make critical decisions about your future.

It does not really matter whether you agreed to separate by mutual consent or if one of you has decided to end your relationship. There is pain on all sides.

Yet, you still have lives to lead, decisions to make and futures to build. If you have children who are minors or have special needs, you need to plan for ongoing parenting. If you have property and debts, you need to decide how to divide what you have and what you owe. And, depending on the family's finances, it may be important to figure out the amount of support to be provided. How do you work this out together? How can it be possible to talk to this other person, who you used to know so well, but now you have drifted apart?

While it is not easy, it is possible to find a way forward. There are many divorced couples and families who live positive lives beyond the experience of separation. It may take time and hard work, but you can establish a good and happy life.

You have two big decisions to make. First, how do you want to work out finances and parenting plans with your spouse—negotiation, mediation, collaborative law or litigation? Second, what financial and parenting plans will work best for you and your family?

Try this... Imagine yourself in five years' time talking to a friend:

"We separated five years ago and we..."

Finishing this sentence will help you to think about HOW you want the separation to proceed between you and your partner.

THE PERSONAL EXPERIENCE OF SEPARATING

It is widely recognized that separation is one of the most stressful personal experiences anyone can ever go through. You will probably feel vulnerable, sad, fearful, confused and angry. The feelings you experience during separation and divorce are real and normal. Many health professionals have worked over the years to understand how we respond to such crises and what we can do to help ourselves overcome them.

Elisabeth Kúbler-Ross studied how people deal with grief when faced with a terrible loss. She learned through her research that people go through a number of stages (see the illustration on the next page). This is a generalized description. Your experience may have some of these elements. But, it will be unique.

You might ask why it's helpful to know about these stages of grief and loss. For one thing, while your feelings are unique, everyone experiencing separation and loss goes through the same stages. Second, you can see there is an end, a time when you have moved through all the stages, and are ready to begin your new life. Third, understanding where you are in this transition can help you with your decision-making.

For example, it may be hard to make good decisions when you are depressed, if you are so angry that being in the same room with your spouse is difficult, or if you are in denial and you are having difficulty focusing on making decisions.

If you are too upset to discuss and make decisions about all the issues, maybe you can find a way to settle some things on a temporary basis until you are ready to deal with all the parenting and financial issues.

If you continue feeling overwhelmed, and are having difficulty with the important decisions, consider talking with someone you trust--not to take sides--to listen to you and offer encouragement. Meanwhile, defer the really big decisions until you are able to think more clearly about your future.

Experiences "Our friends didn't really know what was going on but they stopped coming around. He went out with his friends and I went out with mine. They were great. I used to talk about him all the time. My friends said I should stick up for myself. His friends said the same to him. There was one friend who tried to stop us". (To read more real life experiences go to Chapter 6)

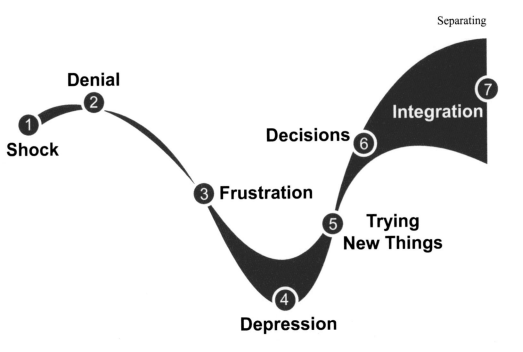

Stage 1: Shock and surprise in response to the event or change. "I can't believe what's happened!"

Stage 2: Denial of change and finding ways to prove that it isn't happening. Sticking your head in the sand and reassuring yourself that it isn't really happening.

Stage 3: Weighed down with emotions. Experiencing anger, frustration and apathy. Tending to blame everyone and lash out at them. Not ready to accept the reality of the separation.

Stage 4: Hitting rock bottom and experiencing depression and apathy. Everything seems pointless.

Stage 5: Beginning to realize that you need to pull yourself together and take action to take care of yourself and your children. This is where you will start to try out new things.

Stage 6: Making decisions. Figuring out what works and what doesn't. Accepting change and beginning to feel more optimistic and hopeful.

Stage 7: At this stage, you have begun to integrate the new circumstances into your life so that it becomes part of your norm – the new you. Many people use the term "acceptance" for this stage.

SEPARATING: A TIME OF CHANGE

The challenge of dealing with so many issues that come with separation and divorce is usually very unsettling. Even if you know that separating is the right decision, it is a time of turmoil. The trail of anger and sadness is very far away from the optimism and joy of the marriage ceremony.

How you deal with these changes can be affected by how you handled crises in the past. There is a sense of increased vulnerability but we can draw on our past to help us at this time.

You may not be able to alter what's happening, but you do have a choice about how you cope with it. You can stay bitter and sad, allowing the separation to control your life. Or, you can find a way to make the best you can of these changes—even if you want to resist them. You can choose to learn new ways to cope and, ultimately, you can build a better future for yourself and your children.

If you handle the crisis well, then no matter how painful or confusing it was, you will be able to make a good life for yourself.

Experiences "When my marriage finished, I felt lost. I was on my own. We had been together for 15 years and a lot of those had been good.

My lawyer said it would help me if I handled my own affairs, so I sorted out my own bank accounts and bills. It was a bit daunting at first but I began to enjoy managing my own life.

I could have relied on my lawyer to sort out the separation but he told me that this would not help me in the long run. I followed his advice and it has worked.

We finally agreed on our divorce this month and I felt confident about going into court. We have a good agreement and I think we managed to be fair to each other. I didn't get everything I wanted but, then, neither did my husband, so I suppose that counts as fair.

Anyway, I walked out of court knowing that I was okay on my own. I could take charge of my life. I liked that."

HOW WE MAKE DECISIONS

Quite often we hear people talking about making "rational decisions" or leaving "feelings to one side". We can't do this. Our brains are wired to take feelings into account. Especially in divorce, feelings always matter when you are making decisions.

You and your partner can't make choices about parenting arrangements unless each of you takes into account your love for your children and your feelings about being a parent.

Even discussions about financial matters are affected by your emotions. Your decisions about property and support may be influenced by your feelings about financial security or your anxiety about having enough for you and your children.

Allowing your emotions to get the best of you, instead of managing them, leads to decision-making that can be just as dangerous and unrealistic as believing you can be completely rational while ignoring your emotions.

What you need is a healthy balance of emotion and reason.

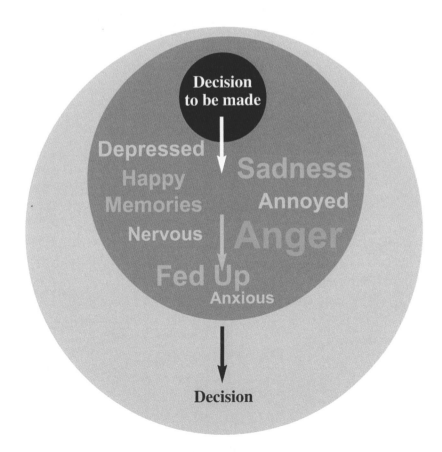

5

WE FEEL BEFORE WE THINK...

It's nearly impossible to separate thinking and emotions. Some of us are better at objective reasoning skills. Some of us rely on a feeling-based approach. Both methods are important. Thinking and feeling are both necessary in making sound and practical choices.

You have many important decisions to make. Think carefully, and base your decisions on good information. Because you have an emotional history with your partner, your feelings will also play an important role in making those decisions.

CHECKLIST FOR DECISION-MAKING
You will find additional information on Negotiation and Decision-Making on pages 18, 19.
1. Make a list of what you need to decide. You may want help from an attorney or other professional to be sure your list is complete.
2. Do any of these issues bring up strong emotional reactions? Which ones?
3. Can you think clearly about the issues, or do your emotions overwhelm you? Can you find a good balance between thinking and feeling?
4. Decide if you can talk with your spouse about some or all of these issues.
5. Set some basic ground rules if you do talk together (take frequent breaks, no name-calling, stick to one issue at a time, focus on the task not the hurts and misunderstandings from your marriage).

Try this...

1. Draw a picture of where you live (it does not need to be a masterpiece!).
2. Write down on the page all the feelings you have about this place.
3. Write beside the picture the decisions you may need to make about it.
4. Can you sense your feelings as you write down each possible decision?
5. Which feelings are helpful and which are clouding your vision?

ANXIETY IN DECISION MAKING

Sometimes, when you feel emotionally overwhelmed, you might reach a tipping point. Your system floods with adrenaline and the thinking part of your brain may take a back seat. You might freeze or have difficulty thinking straight. When this happens, you may feel confused, become anxious, go blank and may even start to sweat.

At the very point you need to be at your best in order to make smart choices, you may feel panicked and unable to cope.

This is a real and common reaction. When it happens, it can floor us. How many times have you looked back on a discussion and thought, "If only I had kept my cool?" or "If only I had said that instead?" It happens to all of us. But, you don't have to be controlled by these feelings.

So what can you do? All performers prepare before sports events or concerts. This helps them focus on their performance, and allows them to stay cool in the heat of the moment. Before an important conversation, be prepared. Take time to think about what you want, what might happen, and how you want to act. This may also be a good time to decide whether you want to do this on your own or whether you want help, perhaps from an attorney.

Before the meeting, ask yourself these questions:

> 1. What do I expect of myself in this meeting?
>
> 2. What do I expect of the other person?
>
> 3. What are my goals?
>
> 4. What do I need to do to fulfill these goals?
>
> 5. What do I think the goals of the other person will be?
>
> 6. What information will I need and how do I need to prepare?
>
> You may even want to write the answers to these questions.

If you know you have something important to say in the discussion, write it down and practice several times in the mirror beforehand. You may even want to try out different ways of saying it and think of how the other person might respond. Now practice what you might say to those responses.

Things may not go exactly as you imagined. That's natural. Don't worry. Rehearsing will give you confidence. You will have a chance to fine-tune what you want to say. If you rehearse, you will be ready for almost anything that comes up.

In the meeting:

If you feel anxious, slow down. Take three deep breaths. Focus on staying calm. Or take a break. Then respond.

After the meeting, ask yourself:
1. What did I do well?

2. What could I have done better?

3. Do I feel alright?

4. If not, what would help me at the moment?

After this, take time to relax. Do something you enjoy, before returning to your daily routine.

Try this...

1. Keep a notebook with you and after every discussion write down your thoughts about what happened, the issues that are important to you and your feelings about what you said and how you responded to the other person.
2. Build up a record that you can use to map your progress.
3. Look back at your notes before you go to your next meeting.
4. Decide how you will take care of yourself in the next discussion.

WHY DO I HAVE TO BE THE REASONABLE ONE?

So, you are reading this and thinking, "I can do all of this but I am not the unreasonable one here!" Maybe that is true. But, you can only manage yourself. You can't force your spouse to change. In fact, the more you try, the less success you'll have.

It can be so frustrating to feel as if you are constantly on the receiving end of someone's unreasonable behavior. Nothing you do seems to make the situation easier. You feel as if you give in to keep the peace. If this is your situation, stay calm. Do not lose your cool.

Stay focused on your goals. Keep the discussion centered on topics, facts and decisions. Don't get lost in your reactions to each other. It's often easy to fall into old patterns and arguments.

Be realistic about your expectations. This is new territory for you. These discussions take time.

If things get really difficult and you can't make progress, then get support from family, friends, or your clergy. This would be a good time to decide whether you need advice from an attorney.

Here is a simple checklist to help you make smart and successful decisions.

1. Smart decisions come from good information. Make sure you have all the documents and other materials you need.
2. Prepare—think about your goals.
3. Pick a time and place when you can talk without distraction for at least an hour. No kids around.
4. Choose one topic to begin and stay on that topic until you reach a decision or until you feel it's best to move onto another topic.
5. If you disagree, see if you can work it through. Use the SALT process on pages 20-21.
6. Don't become distracted. It's easy to get into the cycle of blame and bitterness. Keep your attention on the topic.
7. See if you can create more than 2 options—yours and theirs. Try to find a solution that works for both of you.
8. Evaluate the alternatives. The key question to answer is: "Will this work?"
9. Choose the alternative that seems most workable and reasonable. Then ask, "How will we know if this is working?"

SEPARATION: A JOINT EXPERIENCE

You may feel as if you no longer have anything in common with your spouse. The truth is you created a family together, you still have a relationship - even if it is currently filled with bitterness instead of love. No one knows your family like the two of you. And now you need each other to negotiate a mutually satisfactory, fair and equitable agreement.

The more you argue about each issue, without focusing on practical solutions, the more unsolvable it can become. And, you can get more bitter and frustrated.

When you spend time focusing on the hurt you feel, anger builds up and thoughts become more intense. You become more convinced you are right. Forgiveness is out of the question and revenge can seem more important than solutions. You feel entitled to your positions. Your attitude can become holier-than-thou. The only problem is... the same thing is happening to your partner.

If you decide to fight every step of the way, then you have to accept that your spouse will react in the same way. Maybe there is good reason for you to be annoyed but, when it comes to negotiating your separation, realize you cannot force your spouse to change. Instead, you need to think about what you can control - your own behavior and how it is affecting the decisions about your separation.

The level of crisis you feel is all part of separating. It's natural and understandable. Despite bitterness, sadness and disappointment, you still have a choice in how you behave.

The truth is, if you want things to be fair, then you have to be fair yourself. This doesn't mean you should do all the compromising, or that you should give up something you really believe in. What it does mean is that you don't let your anger or desire for revenge control the discussion.

The reality is that the person you are fighting with is the person who can have a powerful impact on how your separation will work out. You are in this together.

And, if you both realize this--that you need each other to make smart decisions—you might want to try mediation or collaborative law. These approaches help you and your spouse work together to find the most effective and practical solutions.

Try this...

1. Think about the biases and assumptions you have about your spouse.
2. Do these assumptions affect how you feel about your spouse?
3. Think about the assumptions your spouse may have about you.
4. How are assumptions about each other affecting your ability to work together to find solutions?
5. What does this mean for any future agreement?
6. Could you think of things differently and how would that help?

Don't lose sight of the fact that you have some control over your life and you have a future to build.

CAN WE TALK?

Asking this question may often be met with sarcasm and laughter. "If we were able to talk we wouldn't be in this situation!" At the same time, there are important issues to be dealt with and they will have to be sorted out one way or another. And, talking together is the most efficient and effective way to create workable solutions.

It is easy to think that handing all the difficult conversations and decisions over to someone else is the best thing to do and that it would cut out the arguments, hurtful comments or long silences. Some people hire lawyers to do that for them. Others prefer to let a judge decide. Take time to think what's the wisest choice for you and your family.

Don't give up just because things are hard.

When things get difficult, you may want to hire an attorney to speak for you. Sometimes this is the best thing you can do for yourself. Like all your decisions, this is important. Sometimes, you need someone to be your advocate. But, even if you hire a lawyer, remember that you are in charge. The attorney can give you excellent advice, provide essential information, and speak on your behalf.

It would be wonderful if spouses could just talk and resolve or manage the divorce issues. And, you should try. Maybe you can work things out together.

In the end no one knows what you and your family need better than you. No one understands your financial situation or your children and their needs better than you. Whether you talk directly with your spouse, or you hire an attorney, remember: you are in charge. No one understands your financial situation or your children and their needs better than you.

Try this...
Think about what you and your spouse need to discuss.
1. If you are concerned that the conversation will get heated, find a "neutral" place to meet, like a coffee shop or other public place.
2. Decide beforehand, and make an agenda: - What you are going to discuss, such as finances or parenting plan. - How long the meeting will last.
3. Keep the discussion focused and time-limited. Don't try to cover too much; you can always have another meeting. Small successes make a big difference.
4. Make an agreement in advance to treat each other with respect.

CAN YOU DO THIS YOURSELF OR DO YOU NEED A THIRD PARTY?

This idea of talking with your spouse can seem like a big task, but, if there are issues to sort out, there are a number of basic choices as to how to do this:

Mediator: Helps couples negotiate and come up with solutions that are workable for them. The mediator is an impartial third person and does not make decisions for the parties. The mediator is a conflict resolution professional who can provide useful information and help the parties focus on the issues even when they are emotional. Can write up a mediated agreement.

Collaborative lawyer: Represents you and acts on your behalf in one or a series of meetings with your spouse and his/her collaborative lawyer. A mental health professional and/or financial professional is often involved in order to provide helpful information, constructive advice, and options for decision-making. Everyone in this process is committed to finding workable solutions by sharing information, resolving differences in a cooperative manner, and working together to help you and your spouse make smart, practical and fair decisions. The collaborative lawyer does not represent you in related litigation requiring a trial or other contested court process.

13

Attorney: A family lawyer can provide legal advice; offer opinions about what may happen in court; help you gather information; suggest options for settling the divorce; guide you through the legal process; and represent you in Court. The attorney may also attend and assist you in mediation, or be part of the collaborative process.

Judge: Listens to evidence and arguments from both sides and makes a final decision based on legal arguments and the facts put before him or her. Judges also consider the credibility of witnesses and evidence, decide what testimony is legally relevant and admissible, and use their own discretion to determine the outcome.

Remember: Asking a judge to make decisions about your family means that the decisions are no longer in your hands.

DO YOU THINK YOU CAN MAKE DECISIONS TOGETHER?

If you and your spouse can talk and make decisions together, then you can probably sort out most of the issues involved in your separation.

You and your spouse are the experts on your own lives. You know better than anyone else what can work and what makes sense. The best agreements happen when you and your spouse work together.

Decide whether you and your spouse can make joint decisions about the divorce. Think about how you were able to make decisions in the past.

1. Can you think of a time when the two of you made a difficult decision together?
    - How did you do it? What did it take?
    - What did each of you contribute?
    - What did each of you do well?

2. Is it possible to use this past experience to help you work together now?

3. Answer these questions to help you and your spouse decide whether the two of you can talk together, discuss issues and make good agreements:
    - Can you voice what matters to you?
    - Can you say what you need and what bothers you?
    - Can you be heard? Will your spouse listen to you?
    - Can you accept that your spouse also has issues that matter?
    - Can you accept that your spouse also needs to speak and be listened to?

For some couples, working together isn't possible. They can't talk to each other easily. There is a history of abuse or violence. They just aren't able to work together. If that's you, then hire a professional—mediator, collaborative lawyer or attorney—who can assist you.

Remember:
- The best results happen when spouses make decisions together. That way, you stay in control of what happens in your life.
- No matter who helps you—a mediator or an attorney—you and your spouse will make the decisions that affect your future.

HOW DO YOU TALK TO EACH OTHER?

At what point can both of you come to an agreement on all the issues involved in your separation? It might help you to think about how you made decisions in the past.

1. When things were good, how did you and your spouse make decisions? Did you make them together or did you each have areas of responsibility?

2. When you had a disagreement, what happened? How did you patch things up?

3. Can you think of a time when the two of you made a difficult but good decision? How did you do it?
   What did each of you contribute?
   What did each of you do well?

4. Is it possible to use past experiences of making good decisions together now?

What are you both likely to agree on?

   - If you have children, what would they appreciate most about any agreement you make?
   - What can you do or say to help your family move toward an agreement that works for you and your family?
   - What can your spouse do or say to help your family move toward a fair agreement?
   - What would you be prepared to offer to your spouse to reach a fair agreement?
   - What do you think your spouse might offer to reach an acceptable agreement?

So, what are the main things that have to be decided at this time?

They are the same matters you have been dealing with during your marriage:
   - Where to live.
   - How to manage money.
   - How to raise the children.
   - How to pay for their food, clothing, education, health and welfare.
   - How to prepare for old age.
   - How to make good decisions about assets and debts.

Now you are changing the way you and your partner manage these matters.

Remember that you are the expert on your own life. You know more than anyone else about what makes you happy, how to parent your children, how to manage your finances, and how you want to live your life. No matter who helps you - it will be you and your spouse who finally decide on the most practical and reasonable solutions.

NEGOTIATION 101

We all negotiate. Every one of us uses negotiation skills every day. We use negotiation when we talk with our spouse about whether we can afford to replace our aging car. When we talk about whether to let our 12-year old child have a cell phone, we are negotiating. At work, we use negotiation when we bargain with a boss or supervisor about work hours, job assignments and pay. Negotiation is even involved when we work out differences with neighbors about the location of a fence.

A simple definition of negotiation: when people who have different ideas about how to solve a problem hold discussions, exchange proposals and come to a mutually agreeable solution.

For some it comes naturally, and for others, it takes planning and effort. If you want to negotiate with your spouse—either over the "kitchen table" or with the help of a mediator or collaborative lawyer, these tools will help you be successful.

1. Prepare. Success always depends on being prepared. That means:
  a. Gather necessary financial information and documents.
     Be sure you have the information described on pages 51, 53 and 55.
  b. Be sure you have what you need to talk about parenting. Gather information such as your children's school calendar and the schedule of their activities; their child care needs; and work schedules for you and your spouse.
  c. If you decide to consult with an attorney or other professional, do this before meeting with your spouse.
  d. Find a time when you won't be interrupted and a location where you can talk freely, and give yourselves at least an hour.

2. Make a plan. Decide in advance, if possible, what topic or topics you will discuss and how long you will meet. Keep to one topic until you reach agreement or decide to put that issue aside for a while.

3. Think about what you want and what you need. These are not always the same. Need is your bottom line; want is your wish list. Don't aim too high or set the bar too low.

4. **Consider starting with the easier topics first,** issues where you are likely to find common ground. Doing this can increase your confidence, give you positive experience and build momentum for tackling more difficult issues.

5. **Manage your expectations.** It's good to have high hopes. It's also important to be realistic. These conversations can take time. There will probably be ups and downs. That's normal. Keep your goal in mind--a practical, realistic and effective plan.

6. **Manage your emotions.** Talking with your spouse after separation can be emotional—that's completely natural and expected. Talking about your children and your finances can also be emotional. The trick in these discussions is to make sure your emotions don't control you. It's OK to feel strongly, be frustrated, confused, anxious, or even relieved. For helpful tips, see page 46.

7. **Ask questions—and listen carefully.** When you learn what your spouse thinks, feels, and why, you can figure out how to present your own ideas. Encourage your spouse to ask you questions to draw out as much information as possible, so together you can make smart decisions. See the list of helpful questions on pages 20 and 21.

8. **Give yourself a break.** Sometimes, things get heated or confused. You or your spouse get frustrated. The thought going through your head could be, "How will this ever work?" "This will never work." It's OK to just stop. You don't need to make this a marathon. Take a break. Or, stop and pick a date and time when you will begin again. See the SALT process on pages 20 and 21 for how to deal with a disagreement.

There will be times when you and your spouse disagree and it seems you can't make any progress—in fact, it may seem that you'll never be able to resolve your differences. Everyone has those moments—it's a natural part of working toward an agreement. It may not be easy, and it may not be pleasant, but you can get through these disagreements if you pour a little SALT on the discussion.

SALT

SALT is a simple and easy to follow method for dealing with those difficult times when you and your spouse reach a standstill.

Stop

1. Are things getting too "hot"? Is there a risk we will simply argue and not come up with solutions?

2. Do I or does my spouse need to cool down?

3. Would it be good to take a time out in order to think clearly?

4. Do we need to stop so we can collect more pieces of information?

Ask

1. What are your concerns? Then you can state your own.

2. What do we each want to accomplish? Are we getting there?

3. Are we in agreement on what we want to talk about?

4. What can each of us do to help us work out our differences?

5. How do we get back on track?

6. Do we have all the information we need?

7. Are we able to continue? If not, when should we talk again?

Listen

1. Listen to what your spouse is saying.

2. Ask your spouse to listen to you too.

3. Look at your spouse's body language—what is it telling you? And, what is your body language saying?

4. Pay attention to your feelings and the feelings of your spouse.

5. Do not interrupt. Take turns.

6. If you're thinking about your response to your spouse, you won't really be hearing what she/he is saying.

Talk

1. Talk with each other—not over each other, not at each other.

2. What would you like to happen now? Then state what you would like.

3. Focus on problem solving— what are some mutually acceptable solutions?

4. Finger pointing and blaming won't solve conflicts, it only makes them worse.

5. Talking helps you clear up misunderstandings and gives you more information for making smart choices.

BEING AT THE KITCHEN TABLE

How do you get from disagreement to solutions? How do you turn arguments into agreements?

1. **State your own needs and interests.** Know what you want, and your reasons. You can't expect someone to read your mind. You need to be able to tell your partner, very clearly, what you are thinking and why. See the chart, Options, on page 23.

2. **Listen to what matters to your spouse.** Listen carefully, even in the middle of a conflict or argument. If you understand what she/he wants and why, you can give a better response—either agreeing or disagreeing.

3. **Communicate effectively.** Communication is a two-way process. It involves speaking clearly on your own behalf and listening to the other person.

4. **Focus on solving the problem.** The constant cycle of arguing and blaming keeps you from moving ahead. Try this simple and proven method:

   (i)   Prepare: Make sure you have all the information you will need.
   (ii)   Pay attention to the problem, not the person: Seeing your spouse as the problem won't help.
   (iii)   Be willing to consider alternatives: When you seem to be at a road-block, use brainstorming to find alternative solutions. Or follow the SALT approach, see page 20 and 21.
   (iv)   Think clearly: Use common sense standards to evaluate the options. Don't just do what your brother did in his divorce, or think that you should ask for what your best friend received in their divorce.
   (v)   Reality-check the choices: Which ones will truly solve the problem and work.
   (vi)   Before you call it quits: Don't let emotions or frustration keep you from reaching an agreement. What will happen if you can't reach an agreement? It's easy to say, "Let the judge decide," but is that really the answer?
   (vii)   Act: Make a decision that really solves the problem.

5. **Make the agreement work.** A good agreement is realistic, practical and will last. There is no point in agreeing to something that is not likely to work, just to end the fight. One of the most important questions to ask yourself is "Will it work?"

When you and your spouse can make your own decisions, when you find solutions that suit you and your family, your agreements will work.

- If we keep talking, could I learn something that might be useful?
- If we keep talking, might she/he listen and learn something that could be helpful?
- Can I say something that would be helpful?
- What do I want my spouse to say so we can keep working toward an agreement?
- If we can work this out, what will my life be like?
- If we can't reach an agreement, what will happen?
- What is the cost of continuing to talk?
- What could I gain by trying to sort this out now?

Options:

Identify and prioritize possible options (do one chart for yourself and another for what you think are the options and priorities for your spouse):

	Family home	Parenting	Child Support	Spousal Maintenance	Assets and Debts
My preferred option:					
This is acceptable:					
I could live with:					
I would rather not:					

What are you both likely to agree on?

If you have children, what would they appreciate most about any agreement you and your spouse make?

What can you do or say to help your family reach a mutually acceptable agreement?

What can your spouse do or say to help reach a mutually acceptable agreement?

What would you be prepared to offer your spouse to reach such an agreement?

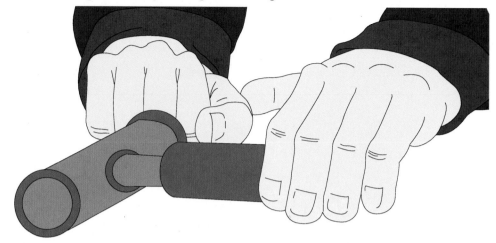

DIVORCE

When you marry, you form a legal union with your spouse that is governed by California laws. If you want to end that union, it has to be done through a legal process.

[Many of the same issues that apply to married couples also apply to unmarried couples. You can find additional information about separation and divorce in the Tool Box section.]

You and your spouse, or the Court if you can't agree, must make decisions about parenting, child support, division of assets and debts and spousal support.

Among the issues you will need to resolve (or ask the court to determine), include:

• parenting your children, including time sharing and responsibility for making decisions for your children about education, medical care and other important aspects of their lives;

• child support; how you and your spouse will make sure your children have what they need from clothing to food, and from health care to haircuts;

• dividing assets and debts, including pensions and retirement accounts; and

• payment of spousal support, if appropriate.

WHERE CAN I FIND MORE INFORMATION ABOUT DIVORCE AND SEPARATION IN CALIFORNIA?

In the Tool Box section of this book, you will find links to many useful resources to help you with your separation and divorce. You will be able to learn about divorce and find all the forms you will need if you decide to handle the divorce on your own. You will be able to learn about child support guidelines, parenting plans, Social Security, retirement plans, and many other very important topics.

For those who want to use an attorney to help them with the separation and divorce, there are links in the Tool Box section both to the State Bar of California which operates a referral service and to legal services programs for those unable to afford a lawyer.

Here are some helpful guidelines if you decide to talk with an attorney.

Who do I go to for legal advice?

The person you need to consult is a family law attorney. You may also want to ask whether the attorney practices collaborative law and whether she/he regularly helps clients in mediation. Be clear and honest. With good and complete information the attorney can give you good advice. When you schedule the appointment, ask what information you should bring.

What will the attorney need to know?

- The date and place of marriage.
- Names and dates of birth of your children.
- Employment information for you and your spouse, including several recent pay stubs for both of you, if possible.
- Financial information, such as bank statements, income tax returns, information about any retirement plans and accounts, list of valuable assets, list of your expenses and debts (including copies of recent bills and credit card statements). Copies of any agreements you have already made with your spouse (before marriage, during marriage, or after separation) and court orders and judgments.

How much will it cost?

Legal fees vary and it will depend on what the attorney needs to do on your behalf, the complexity of issues involved, level of conflict, expectations of you and your spouse, and which process is used. Specifically ask the attorney about "unbundled legal services." When you make the initial appointment, ask about the fees and costs. Lawyers are obliged to give you a written statement of their fees. They may also give you an estimate of the total fees and costs. If you cannot afford an attorney, there may be legal aid programs or volunteer lawyer groups where you can get low-cost or free advice. The State Bar of California is a good resource for finding an attorney, including lawyers who will provide a free or reduced price consultation. Information about finding an attorney can be found in the Tool Box section of this book and on the website created for this book.

What does an attorney do?

After gathering essential information, your attorney will advise you on your legal rights and obligations. Based on your decisions about the role you want the attorney to play, he or she can represent you in court proceedings, accompany you to mediation or collaborative law meetings, advise you with regard to settlement options, and draft any legal documents.

Divorce Coaching

A divorce coach can help you before seeking a divorce, during the divorce process, and/or after your divorce. It all depends upon your particular needs.

Divorce coaches don't offer legal advice; they are not your therapist or financial advisor. However, divorce coaches are professionals who are licensed or certified in divorce-related fields. For more information about the training and certification of divorce coaches, see information in the Tool Box.

A divorce coach will help you organize your thoughts, assist you to collect the documents you will need, and help you set your priorities. Coaches help improve and streamline communication with your spouse, attorney, mediator, and other divorce professionals.

A divorce coach can help you decide whether to file for divorce. If you go ahead, a coach can help you figure out which other professionals, if any, to hire and which model of divorce (kitchen table, collaborative, mediated or litigated) is best for you.

During the divorce process, a divorce coach will help you locate helpful resources, decide your priorities, and locate and understand documents you'll need. And, the coach will assist you to set goals and follow through on them.

After divorce, a coach can help you make sure the parenting plans work, help you with your finances, and in general help you move forward with your new life.

WHICH PROCESS WILL WORK BEST FOR YOU?

As we mentioned previously, there are basically four ways to resolve the parenting and financial issues in your divorce.
• discussions between you and your spouse (kitchen table)
• family mediation
• collaborative practice
• traditional court process
Sometimes couples or individuals will use more than one of these methods in order to achieve a settlement.

Choose the approach that's right for you. You will find good information in this book, and there are many references in the Tool Box that will help you learn about all the methods. The following are a few questions that might help you make your decision:
• Do you want to be directly involved?
• Can you and your spouse work together to any extent?
• For each method, what would be expected of you? How much time and effort would be required?
• What are the likely costs for each method? Are there reduced fee services available (for example, court-based mediation, legal aid)?
• Do you know professionals who could help you (attorney, financial professional, counselor)?
• What types of advice or information do you need to make good decisions?
• Do you need help gathering information and making sense of it?
• Do you feel you need someone to speak for you?
• How long does each method take to complete?

Ask friends and family members for recommendations. If at all possible, interview more than one professional. Some may offer a reduced fee for an initial consultation.

MEDIATION

How can mediation help?

Mediators help when you and your spouse are having problems talking with each other so you can figure out what's best for you and your family.

The goals of mediation are: help you work together; determine what you need to discuss in terms of parenting and finances; make sure you have all the information you need; talk about ways to handle your finances and parent your children; work with you to resolve disagreements; and make fair, practical and reasonable decisions.

The mediator is a guide who helps you figure out what's right, not a judge who will tell you what to do. You and your spouse decide what you think is right for your family.

How does mediation work?

The mediator meets with you and your spouse. There can be one or several meetings. That usually depends on the number of issues to resolve. Often you meet together with the mediator, but sometimes it's better if you and your spouse are in different rooms and the mediator meets with each of you separately. Mediation meetings usually last for two or more hours—how long is up to the two of you and the mediator. If you have an attorney, then she or he can attend the mediation.

It's important to know that mediation is private and confidential. Nothing you or your spouse says in mediation can ever be brought up in court. The mediator cannot be called as a witness.

The **first** step in mediation is to come up with a list of the issues you want to address, such as parenting your children, the amount of child support and any other expenses for your children, how to deal with your assets and debts, what to do with any pensions and whether spousal support should be paid. The mediator will help you make sure you talk about all the possible topics so any agreement will be complete and comprehensive.

The **second** step is to be sure you have complete and accurate information. You can't make good decisions without having all the necessary documents and other pieces of information. For example, to work out a parenting plan, you probably should have the schedules for the children's school or day care, and for any other activities such as athletics and music. When you talk about child support, you should have information about all sources of income as well as an accurate picture of expenses for each of you and for your children.

The **third** step is problem-solving—trying to find practical solutions and plans that

28

work for your family. The mediator's job at this point is to help you and your spouse talk with and listen to each other. Good communication is essential to good problem-solving. To do this the mediator will ask questions and help you listen to each other. Sometimes these conversations can become emotional and frustrating. Mediators are skilled at helping you keep talking even when you can't seem to get an agreement and things seem hopeless.

There are probably many things on which you and your spouse agree. But there will also be disagreements. This is natural. Don't be discouraged. For example, you may have one idea for a time schedule with the children and your spouse has a very different suggestion. Mediators help you talk cooperatively about these disagreements, even when you might be very frustrated. They help you look for ways to work out your differences, including finding alternatives that neither of you had considered. This is part of the mediator's role.

Many times, mediation is conducted with everyone in the same room. This allows you to talk directly with your spouse. Sometimes, it makes sense to take a break and have separate meetings with the mediator. These individual conversations are confidential, and the mediator will not tell the other person anything you said, unless you tell them to do so.

The **fourth** step is working out an agreement. Most mediations end with a written document that sets out the plans you and your spouse have agreed to. This is sometimes called a Memorandum of Understanding or MOU. The MOU is then converted into a Settlement Agreement which can be prepared by the mediator or an attorney. The MOU is incorporated into the parenting plan and/or property agreement and becomes part of the Judgment for Dissolution of Marriage. Once the Settlement Agreement is approved and signed by you and your spouse, it is submitted to the Court for final approval.

Why consider mediation?

1. You make the decisions, not a judge. You choose what's best for your family. When you decide, the results are better for you and your family.
2. Couples who make decisions together are more likely to live up to them—they make their agreements work. And, they tend to be long-lasting.
3. Couples who work together learn to problem-solve. This helps them when they face new situations that require cooperation.
4. Mediation helps promote good communication and cooperation. Couples who participate in mediation are frequently able to gain trust and reduce bitterness.
5. Resolving conflicts helps your children. The greatest source of continuing emotional stress for children is parental conflict. Mediation helps parents reduce and even eliminate their conflicts.

COLLABORATIVE DIVORCE

How does it work?

Each spouse hires a family law attorney who has specialized training as a collaborative lawyer. The overall objective is for the spouses and their lawyers to work cooperatively to create practical and realistic solutions to the issues in the divorce. Instead of acting as adversaries, collaborative lawyers work in a cooperative manner in order to help the spouses. To do this, they provide advice to their clients, make sure there is full, complete and accurate information, help the spouses understand the information, assist them to talk about how they want to handle their finances and parent their children, and seek a set of agreements acceptable to the spouses.

At the start, the spouses, attorneys, and other collaborative professionals, sign a participation agreement. As part of this agreement, everyone commits to a cooperative approach. They agree to share information freely and frankly and work together to find fair and reasonable solutions. They also agree that if the collaborative process fails, the lawyers and other collaborative professionals will not participate in a contested court proceeding.

Occasionally, professionals (such as a financial planner, child specialist and divorce coach) are asked to join the group in order to interpret information, offer opinions, and make recommendations.

What is the difference between collaborative practice and mediation?

In mediation, the parties are assisted by a neutral third party to make their own decisions. In collaborative practice, there is no third party to help manage the discussions. The lawyers use their legal knowledge, training as collaborative professionals, and experience as practical negotiators to assist their clients to negotiate workable parenting and financial plans. Once an agreement (MSA) is reached, the lawyers take all necessary steps to complete the divorce process.

What kind of information and documents do I need to provide?

You need to collect the same information no matter what process you use— negotiation, mediation, collaborative practice or litigation. In the Tool Box section, you will find a link to relevant websites where you will find all the documents you will need, including guidelines, a child support calculator, forms for parenting plans, and financial affidavits where you list income, expenses, assets and debts.

COURT (LITIGATION) ROUTE

How does it work?
Hearings in court, before a magistrate or judge, are scheduled. Each party presents evidence—testimony and documents—and is subject to cross-examination by the other attorney. Often, only the parties give evidence. In some situations, you will need testimony from financial experts or child specialists. Your lawyer will also present legal arguments to support your positions.

After considering all the testimony and documents, the laws and legal rules, and comments from the lawyers, the judge makes a decision that is binding on both parties. Often, one of you gets what you wanted and the other spouse feels cheated, deprived or unfairly treated.

For further information on the court process in California, see the Tool Box section.

What is different about this method?
Your statements—called testimony—are given in response to questions from your lawyer.

There is no direct communication between you and your spouse. You don't have the chance to argue your own position, your lawyer does this for you. The process is formal and structured around court rules and procedures.

Pros and Cons of going to court
This is a general list of some of the advantages and disadvantages of litigation. Your situation is unique, so be sure to talk with your attorney about her/his reasons for recommending that you go to court.

Litigation: tends to be a more expensive process than negotiation, mediation and collaborative practice and generally takes longer. Trial is adversarial - you and your spouse each believe you are right and the other is wrong. Litigation can make conflict with your spouse much worse. On the positive side, court is always available to have a judge: determine the issues that you and your spouse have been unable to resolve, provide temporary support, stop your spouse from hiding assets, prevent a parent from taking the children out of the state, and issue domestic violence restraining orders and child protective orders, among other things.

Do all the issues have to go through court?

No. Always remember that family court is meant to be used as a means of last resort. Furthermore, when child custody issues are involved, parties are required to attend Conciliation Court to work with a child custody counselor to attempt to assist them in reaching an agreement on their own. Some counties have recommending counselors and others don't. In recommending counties, if the parties aren't able to resolve their matter in Conciliation Court, the counselor will make a recommendation to the court. For unresolved child custody issues and all other matters, depending upon the county involved, the judge may refer your case to the Daily Settlement Officer, who will try and help you settle your case on the day of your court hearing.

How do I find out more?

The first thing is to consult a family law attorney, who can advise you. If you don't know who to contact, you can find a family law attorney through the lawyer referral services within your county (see a link in the Tool Box section).

When you speak with an attorney, you will need the same information as for negotiation, mediation and collaborative law processes. Generally, you will need to gather information about your family's finances (employment and income, bank records, income tax returns, retirement plan statements, credit cards and other debts (see Chapter 2, Finances) as well as information that will help resolve issues about how you and your spouse will parent your children (see Chapter 4, Your Children).

Representing yourself in Court (acting Pro Per)

You can save yourself a lot of worry and time if you have the right kind of legal advice. But if you can't afford an attorney, or if you just want to handle things on your own, you can act as your own attorney. People who do this are known as Pro Per.

If you and your spouse can agree on everything, then acting Pro Per may be a good choice. You can save money and handle things at your own pace. Family Law Facilitators at the courthouses in California can provide information and services for Pro Per individuals. Facilitators cannot, however, provide legal advice. Help is provided through group workshops and walk in assistance.

Even if you and your spouse want to act as your own attorneys, it is often a good idea to get legal advice so you can be confident that your decisions about parenting your children and handling your finances are consistent with legal principles. Processing the paperwork with the court is the easy part of separation and divorce, so if you and your spouse have a complete agreement, then you could act in Pro Per without too much difficulty.

Acting as your own attorney in a contested case (litigation) is NOT a good idea. If your spouse is represented by an attorney and you are not, you could have a very difficult time and feel that the result is not good for you and your family.

LEGAL TERMS

Parenting Terminology

Parents, whether married or not, have the legal responsibility to look after their children and make decisions for their benefit. In California, the term used is custody. One parent may be granted legal custody. There are two aspects of parental rights and responsibilities:

Legal custody refers to the right and responsibility of a parent to make major life decisions for the child, such as decisions regarding education, non-emergency medical and dental care, religion and travel.

Physical custody refers to the right and responsibility to make decisions affecting the child on a daily basis.

Legal custody and physical custody may be shared by both parents, divided between parents or held solely by one parent.

Visitation refers to the right to spend time with the child. It can include overnight stays, school holidays, and vacations. The parents may agree on arrangements for custody and visitation - called a Parenting Plan. There are links to the forms that comprise the Parenting Plan in California in the Tool Box section."

More detail about arrangements for parenting children can be found in **Chapter 4, Parenting.**

If parents agree on a **Parenting Plan**, it is usually adopted by the court.

But, if an agreement cannot be reached, either parent may ask the court to issue an Order setting forth the parenting schedule and responsibility for making legal decisions about the child(ren). In this regard, courts generally favor arrangements where the children spend time with each parent, and custodial time is only denied if the court believes that would be harmful to the child or if the parent is unable to provide appropriate care and supervision. In special circumstances, courts may order supervised visitation.

Child Support and Spousal/Partner Support Terminology

Generally, there are two types of support agreed to by the couple, or ordered by the court—Child Support and Spousal/Partner Support.

Child Support is a payment from one parent to the other and used to meet the expenses of the dependent/minor children. Child Support is determined by using a computer program that applies the statewide uniform guideline calculation, based upon information such as the number of children, the parenting timeshare percentage, gross incomes of each parent, certain payroll and income tax deductions. Payment is made part of a court order and can be enforced through the court. To find a California Guideline Child Support calculator, see the reference in the Tool Box section.

Spousal/Partner Support is the term given to the payment made by one spouse for the support of the other. Spousal/Partner Support is determined by a number of factors (see the link to California statutes in the Tool Box section). Some of the criteria used include: the length of the marriage, the relative incomes of the spouses, their health and age, their ability to find employment, and whether one party gave up employment to care for the children. To learn more about California's laws regarding Spousal/Partner Support, look for links in Tool Box section. Spousal/Partner Support can be awarded for a limited period of years or for an indefinite period of time and can be paid weekly or monthly, or in a lump sum. Unless agreed otherwise, Spousal/Partner Support ends on the specified date, the death of either party, remarriage of the spouse receiving support, or further order of court, whichever first occurs.

The court may also order temporary spousal/partner support if such payments are necessary while the divorce is pending.

There are special IRS rules for child support. You should be aware of these rules when you negotiate for these payments. See the Tool Box section for links to information about these rules.

Enforcing a Support or Support Order: If a spouse fails to comply with a court order and does not pay the amount awarded by the court, the court can enforce the order. For example, payments can be deducted from a spouse's income pursuant to a court order.

Family Home Terminology

The family residence, in legal terms, is the property (owned or rented) where family members live and which they consider their principal home. If a couple is unable to resolve the question of who remains in the marital home, whether on their own, with a mediator or through their attorneys, either spouse can ask the court to determine who will occupy the residence.

In deciding whether to make this order, the court will consider all of the family circumstances, including the welfare of minor children or a dependent spouse, the family's financial situation and the existence of a domestic violence restraining order. The court order can include:
- Who has the right to live in the marital home and for how long.
- Who must pay for the expenses of the family residence.
- Ownership rights in the marital home and what share each spouse owns.
- Whether and under what circumstances the home must be sold.

The person who has primary care of the children is almost always awarded at least temporary use of the marital residence. The goal is to provide a sense of security and continuity for the children. The use and occupancy of the residence on a more permanent basis will typically be in accordance with its ownership in accordance with property division.

As part of the final divorce order, the court can order that the marital home be sold and the equity divided between the two spouses in designated percentages. It can also award the property to one spouse as part of the equal division of community property, or order that the sale be deferred for a period of time. For a more than temporary deferred sale, the court will consider market conditions.

Judgment for Dissolution of Marriage

A divorce judgment ends the marriage, makes provisions for parenting, allocates assets and debts and provides for financial support. A Judgment for Dissolution of Marriage is obtained either through agreement or judicial determination. In California, the legal grounds for dissolution of marriage are:
- There are irreconcilable differences that have led to the irremediable breakdown of the marriage or domestic partnership, and there is no possibility of saving the marriage or domestic partnership through counseling or other means.
- The court is satisfied that proper arrangements have been made or will be made for parenting your children, financial support, and division of assets and debts.

California has a six-month waiting period from the time that the other spouse was served with the Petition for Dissolution or Marriage or made an appearance in the case. That it's the earliest date in which the court can grant the divorce. The date on which the judgment of dissolution was entered can affect health insurance and income taxes

Pensions and Property Terminology

A pension or retirement account, in addition to the family home, is often one of the family's most valuable assets. You can decide whether to divide this asset and in what proportion, and your decision will be included in a marital settlement agreement. If you cannot agree on how to handle the pension or retirement fund, the court will divide the community property portions of them equally.

Depending on the type of pension or retirement plan being divided, you may need to have a special document known as a **Qualified Domestic Relations Order (QDRO)** prepared by an attorney and signed by the judge. You can find more information on **QDROs** in the Tool Box section.

It is important for you to know the full details of any pension before negotiating any allocation. Each pension and retirement account has its own rules and requirements. Pensions can be very complicated and it is important to get advice from a specialist in pensions before any final decision is made. For more detail on pensions and retirement plans, see Chapter 2, Finances. Also, there are links to helpful websites in the Tool Box section.

DOMESTIC ABUSE

What is domestic abuse?

> *Domestic violence and domestic abuse are behaviors used by one person in a relationship to control the other. Partners may be married, unmarried; heterosexual, gay, lesbian, bisexual or transgender; living together, separated or dating. Domestic violence does not always mean physical harm. Some examples of domestic abuse include:*
> - *name-calling or put-downs*
> - *keeping a partner from contacting their family or friends*
> - *withholding money*
> - *stopping a partner from getting or keeping a job*
> - *threats of physical harm*
> - *sexual assault*
> - *stalking*
> - *intimidation*
>
> -Definition and examples taken from www.domesticviolence.org

How do I plan a separation when I am afraid of my partner's reaction?

The most important thing is for you and your children to be safe. Think—what is the best way forward for you and your children? You can be successful and safe. To do this you must take your time, think clearly, get good advice, make detailed plans, get support from friends or family, and then act.

Talk to a support person. Support groups and counselors are experienced in listening and helping people at a time like this. There are advocacy groups for victims of domestic abuse. You may also want to talk with an attorney before taking any action.

Be smart. Be careful. Make good plans. Be safe.

Can you ask your spouse to leave or is it safer for you to go? If you decide to leave, do you have a safe place? Can you do this on your own? Do you need help from your family? There are domestic violence organizations throughout the state. Some communities have shelters or temporary housing.

Do you have access to money? If not, you may be able to get emergency payments from community groups such as United Way or Salvation Army. You may also be able to get an emergency support order from a Judge. There are helpful links in the Tool Box section.

Can the law help me at this time?

Yes. California has laws designed to help protect people from domestic violence or abuse. The legal action that will be right for you will depend on your own particular circumstances.

Questions you may want to ask include:
- What laws will protect me and my children?
- How will they protect us? Who enforces the laws?
- Do these laws apply to my situation?
- What kinds of protection are available under the laws?
- How long does it take for a court order to be granted?
- Can an order be renewed?
- Does a court order stop my partner from seeing the children?
- Are there people who can help me get ready for court?
- Are there any costs or fees to obtain a court order?
- Will I need a lawyer to help me?

What will happen with parenting in the future?

It can be difficult, often impossible, to negotiate informal arrangements where domestic abuse has been present. It may be necessary to go to court to seek more formal arrangements. It is also possible that because of the nature and extent of the domestic abuse it would not be a good idea for you or your children to have any contact with the offender—at least temporarily. The most important thing is your safety and the safety of your children.

Will mediation help at this time?

Mediation may be suitable for your family but, equally, it may not. Speak with your attorney about mediation or call a mediator in your area to ask if your case is appropriate for mediation. Mediation can be helpful only when there are special arrangements and rules in place to protect you during the mediation and afterwards.

What can I do to make the parenting arrangements as safe as possible?

1. If you are afraid, ask someone else to be with you, such as a friend or family member. Don't be alone with your spouse. You can also call your local family or child visitation center to see what help is available.

2. Arrange the exchange of the children in a public place, even a police station if necessary.

3. Ask the court to order specific arrangements.

ALCOHOL AND DRUG ABUSE

You or your spouse may have a history of drug or alcohol dependence or abuse. The emotional strain of separation and divorce can increase your or your spouse's reliance on these substances to ease stress and make life seem better. However, this is a time when both of you need to have clear heads and be able to make plans (both short-term and longer-term) for your family, yourself and your children. You need to be able to talk clearly about your needs, goals and plans.

If you have children and, as part of the parenting plan, you will be looking after them on your own, you will need to be able to care for them. If there is any doubt that you can do this, because of alcohol or drug dependency, get help and support. Otherwise, you could harm your children and even risk losing your time with them.

If you are worried that your spouse will be unable to take care of the children because of drinking or drug use, it is important to talk about this with your attorney, in mediation, or court proceedings. You can make arrangements as part of a parenting plan to make sure that drugs and alcohol don't create problems for your family.

There are many support agencies that work with people in a non-judgmental and caring way. This support can mean the difference between coping and not coping, especially over the first weeks and months of a separation. You may want to speak with your family doctor or the children's pediatrician, or contact United Way, The Salvation Army, or other social service agencies.

It is important to have a clear head and be able to advocate effectively for your point of view.

CHILDREN AT RISK—CHILD ABUSE OR NEGLECT

It is against the law to harm a child. California has laws and policies to protect every child from harm, even from members of their own family. These are generally called Child Protection Laws.

It is very important to seek help if you are worried that your partner is harming your child/children. There are many organizations that provide help to families. Please see Tool Box section for information on these organizations.

If you need to seek protection from the court for your child/children, the court may prevent contact; or the court can require supervised access, which is where a child only spends time with the parent in question when there is a trusted adult with them. Arrangements for any contact follow a thorough assessment of the circumstances by the court.

The idea that you or your partner may have supervised or limited access to your children is very hard to face. There are no easy answers for anyone when a child is being harmed by one or both of their parents, or indeed when there is an accusation that this might be happening. The safety of your children is paramount. All you can do is seek support from people and agencies you can trust.

Divorce and Separation - A practical guide to making smart decisions

TELLING THE EXTENDED FAMILY

When there is a death, family and friends gather, there is a funeral or memorial service. When someone is ill, family and friends can visit, bring food, send flowers. But, how do family and friends respond when there is a divorce? How do they show their concern and support?

For your family, it can be a difficult time. Who do they support? What do they say? Do they keep in touch with the person they used to be so fond of? Grandparents worry whether they will be able to see their grandchildren. Cousins, aunts and uncles and other family members may take sides.

Your family will be reeling from the news of your separation and divorce. This is a time of family change. Relationships are redefined and expectations altered, and there is no roadmap to help everyone through. Yet, when all is over and the agreement or court order is in place, your family will still be there—as will your spouse's family. There will be birthdays, graduations and weddings, and deciding who will attend is important. Also, your children still need connections with their extended family.

The extended family can be a help at this time, if you set a few simple ground rules.

Try this...

1. When you are ready to tell your family, ask to meet them. Sit down and tell them clearly that you and your partner are separating. You can decide whether to meet people together or separately. It is very important: do not let someone else do this for you!

2. Be clear that you and your children need their support and, for the children's sake at least, you do not want your family to take sides against your spouse. Explain that the separation is difficult for children. They love both their parents, and it will be even harder for them if family members take sides or talk badly about the other parent.

3. Ask for their support, but not their opinions, unless you specifically seek their advice. They will want to help and offer suggestions. But, it can be too much to have family members pushing you one way or another.

4. Tell them that you and your spouse are going to sort out the separation agreement between you and that when you are ready you will let them know how it is going. Ask them to respect your privacy.

WHAT IF YOUR FAMILIES TAKE SIDES?

We cannot always account for how our families respond. Every family member has a unique way of seeing things. And, everyone has a way of making her or his feelings heard. When they offer opinions, advice or criticize your spouse, it just makes things more difficult for you.

What if a family member says angry and hurtful things about your spouse?

You may agree with your family's criticism of your spouse. But, it is destructive when a family member voices anger about your spouse in front of your children. It is difficult when this happens while you are trying to negotiate the terms of an agreement with your spouse. It can be a huge strain on top of everything else you are coping with.

Try this...

1. Ask to meet with the family member in a neutral venue.
2. Talk to them about how important their support is to you and how you appreciate the way they are feeling on your behalf.
3. Describe how their behavior is affecting you and your children and the difficulties it is causing.
4. Ask them to help you by agreeing:
   a) Not to talk about the children's other parent in front of them.
   b) To think about the effect it has on you and the children, when an argument starts at a family event.
   c) To keep any bitter or angry thoughts to themselves.

Experiences "She said that they didn't know what to do. The day I had arrived to their house and blurted out the news she had been shocked. She liked my husband and didn't want to lose him as a son-in-law. She thought that it might pass and we would change our minds".
(read more real life experiences go to Chapter 6)

What if my spouse and my family stop speaking to each other?

The breakdown of the relationship between your spouse and your family is the most common of inter-family difficulties. If these family conflicts arise, it can be particularly hard for both you and your spouse, and especially the children. Particularly if there were warm relationships beforehand. It's hard enough when you no longer can talk to or visit with your spouse's parents or family members. But, it is especially hard if it stops grandchildren spending time with grandparents or aunts, uncles and cousins.

Try this...

1. Talk to your partner. Do you want your children to have good relationships with grandparents and others from both families?

2. What arrangements do you need to put in place to support this?

3. Seek agreement from your own parents not to talk badly about your spouse?

4. Seek agreement from your partner not to talk badly about your parents.

If relationships become strained because of the separation, you may want to use a mediator or family therapist. It can be helpful to have a trained professional work with your family to improve communication and find a resolution.

What do I say to my spouse's family?

There can be sadness—possibly anger and bitterness—from your spouse's family. And, you probably feel the same way. Once the news of the separation is known, it can be so difficult to know what to say or how to act when meeting them in the street or at a family event. You will probably feel close to some of your spouse's family, and you may want to preserve a good relationship with others—for the sake of your children or even for yourself. With these people, it can be a good idea to use the same basic rules that you use with your own family.

Try this...

1. Ask to meet with people in your spouse's family who matter to you and your family. Tell them you want to keep a good relationship with them. Do this as soon as you can after the news of your separation has become known within the family. Do not wait.

2. Be clear with them that your children need their support and ask them to focus on maintaining a good relationship with the children.

3. Tell them you will not talk about your spouse or the divorce to them and ask them to do the same.

The people who care for you don't always know how to be helpful (and how to avoid making things worse). They may need you to tell them just what you need from them.

TRAVELING THE ROAD OF SEPARATION AND DIVORCE

Divorce changes everything. Focusing on the past can be important in order to understand where and how you and your spouse began to drift apart. But, most of what you will face is the future—what will happen to you and to your children. Everyone goes through stages of grief (page 2). At the same time, you will be faced with many decisions. You owe it to yourself to take the time you need, to plan for your family, to imagine your life after divorce.

Try this...

So, here are some suggestions for how to balance grieving (looking at the past) with decision-making (looking toward the future).

1. Don't let grief become the only thing you experience. Spend time every day (maybe 15-30 minutes) thinking about the past. Feel the loss of your marriage and your dreams. Acknowledge that you are anxious, confused, unsettled. Just remember, you have both a future to consider as well as a past to mourn.

2. Take time every day to plan for your future. Use this time to make lists of what you need to accomplish. Use this time to gather information you will need. Use this time to think about the best results you can imagine.

3. Some people talk with a clergyman, counselor, friend or family member. You might also attend meetings of a support group for women and men going through divorce. Please, do not talk with your children about the divorce and your reactions.

4. Make plans to talk with your spouse—whether over "the kitchen table," in mediation, or with your attorneys.

Experiences "My independence is something I am proud of. For a long time I was part of a couple and then, when that stopped, I felt as if my right arm had been taken off. I had to start all over again... but I did!"

"My divorce was ten years ago. I have a new partner, my kids are grown up and life goes on. I look back and almost can't remember what we fought about".
(read more real life experiences go to Chapter 6)

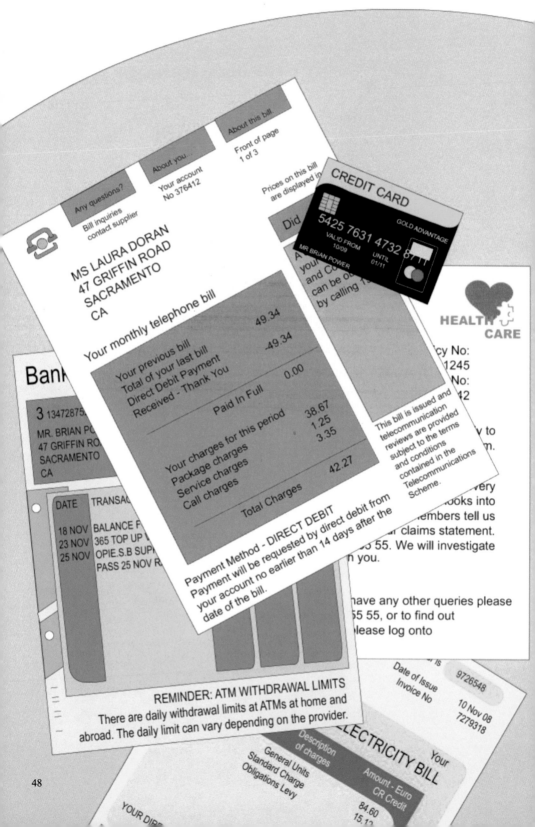

Any questions?

Bill inquiries
contact supplier

About you...

Your account
No 376412

About this bill

Front of page
1 of 3

Prices on this bill
are displayed in

MS LAURA DORAN
47 GRIFFIN ROAD
SACRAMENTO
CA

CREDIT CARD

GOLD ADVANTAGE

5425 7631 4732 8711

VALID FROM
10/09

UNTIL
01/11

MR BRIAN POWER

HEALTH
CARE

Did

A
you
and co
can be o
by calling

cy No:
1245

No:
42

Your monthly telephone bill

Your previous bill	49.34
Total of your last bill	-49.34
Direct Debit Payment Received - Thank You	0.00
Paid In Full	
Your charges for this period	38.67
Package charges	1.25
Service charges	3.35
Call charges	
Total Charges	42.27

This bill is issued and
telecommunication
reviews are provided
subject to the terms
and conditions
contained in the
Telecommunications
Scheme.

Bank

3 134728753

MR. BRIAN PO
47 GRIFFIN RO
SACRAMENTO
CA

DATE	TRANSAC
18 NOV	BALANCE F
23 NOV	365 TOP UP
25 NOV	OPIE.S.B SUPI
	PASS 25 NOV R

Payment Method - DIRECT DEBIT
Payment will be requested by direct debit from
your account no earlier than 14 days after the
date of the bill.

very
ooks into
embers tell us
claims statement.
55. We will investigate
you.

have any other queries please
55 55, or to find out
lease log onto

REMINDER: ATM WITHDRAWAL LIMITS
There are daily withdrawal limits at ATMs at home and
abroad. The daily limit can vary depending on the provider.

Date of Issue
Invoice No

9726548

10 Nov 08
7279318

Description
of charges

General Units
Standard Charge
Obligations Levy

ELECTRICITY BILL

Your
Amount - Euro
CR Credit

84.60
15.12

YOUR DIR

(2)

FINANCES

The most important thing when it comes to the budget for your family is that you have allocated enough money to provide for the children, yourself and to run two homes.

Money

Money is important. You need to make decisions about income and bills, about assets, debts and retirement. Talking about money is important. It's not easy to do, especially during separation and divorce. You can have good discussions about money if you have good information, and you focus on problem solving instead of arguing.

Some of the questions that could come up when you begin to think about finances are:
- Will there be enough?
- How do we make our income cover the cost of two households?
- Will the kids have to give up anything?
- What do we do about our bills and debts?
- What happens to our retirement?
- Where will I live? Will I need to move?
- Can we even afford to get divorced?

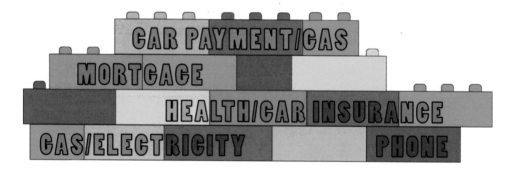

Being uncertain is natural; every couple has anxiety about their finances. But, dealing with these decisions in a positive way can reduce your anxiety.

If dealing with money isn't easy for you, then find someone you can trust—family member, friend or professional—who can help you collect the information, make sense of it, and build a plan for your financial future. You will also find links to helpful websites in the Tool Box section with information on divorce finance decisions.

Don't panic. Take time. Get good information.

HOW DO WE WORK OUT WHAT IS FAIR?

Step 1: Gather Information

We can't stress this enough. Good information leads to good solutions. Here are guidelines for pulling together that information. For all divorce and related court matters, both parties are required to complete a Declaration of Disclosure, which includes a completed Schedule of Assets and Debts, a completed Income and Expense Declaration, and copies of all tax returns filed by you within the prior two years. You will find a link to these forms in the Tool Box section.

In the Income and Expense Declaration you will list:

I. What you earn—each of you
  a) Employment income - shown on pay stubs.
  b) Or, if you are self-employed, a profit and loss statement for the last two years or a Schedule C from your last federal tax return.
  c) Income received from Social Security, and other pension/retirement funds money received for disability, worker's compensation, unemployment or public assistance.
  d) Investment income from: rental properties, stocks and bonds, or trust income.
  e) Money received from any other source—spousal support, gifts from friends or family, inheritance, lottery winnings and such sources.

II. What you owe—jointly or individually
  a) real estate mortgage (and equity loan or second mortgage)
  b) automobile loans (or for motorcycles, boats and other vehicles)
  c) personal loans—anything owed to a lender or to family or friends
  d) credit card balances (the total, not the amount you pay each month)
  e) loans against life insurance policies or retirement accounts

III. What you spend—estimated expenses, actual expenses, or proposed needs. Some of these expenses are:
  a) housing-such as rent, mortgage, taxes, insurance, repairs and maintenance
  b) groceries and household supplies
  c) clothing for yourself and your children
  d) child care, school fees, tuition and other education costs
  e) medical insurance and non-covered medical expenses
  f) other expenses for children, such as allowances, hair cuts, lessons and uniforms
  g) utilities (including cell phone, land line, cable, internet, electric, water, and gas)
  h) other expenses such as eating out, entertainment, charitable contributions, laundry and cleaning, and automobile and transportation expenses.

If you don't know where to find this information, ask your spouse. Or, talk with someone at your bank, your insurance agent or other people who provide financial services for your family. Information is often in your check book, bank statements and credit card statements.

If your spouse has this information and will not share it, talk with an attorney who can obtain a court order to require your spouse to give you all that material.

Make sure your information is up-to-date and accurate.

Step 2: Review the information
If possible, talk with your spouse or present the information to the mediator or your attorney. (see page 6 for helpful ways to talk together)

Each of you, in order to come to a fair agreement, must have a good idea of expenses for your separate households, including your expenses for the children for when they live with you. If you can talk with your spouse, exchange this information directly.

Step 3: What is the overall cost?
Add the expense figures from both budgets. This will give you a total for what it will cost to run both homes. Compare the lists. If there are any expenses that you both listed—count them only once. Look for missing expenses and for items you may want to eliminate or reduce.

Step 4: Joint income
Be sure you have a complete list of your income from all sources. Are there income sources you may have overlooked, especially those that come once or twice a year? Will there be changes in income? Will one of you have a new position or be getting a raise or a bonus? Is one of you returning to work? Will one spouse's work hours be reduced or will they have a reduction in salary?

Step 5: Balancing the budget
Once you have all the information and shared it with your spouse, it's time to talk about how to use your income to meet your expenses.

If your expenses are greater than your income, you will need to be creative in finding ways to balance your budget.
How can the income be used in a smart and practical way?
a) What are the essential expenses?
b) Are there expenses that can be reduced or eliminated?
c) Is there any way of increasing the family income?

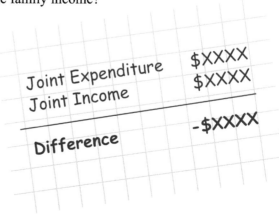

Step 6: How do we work out child support?

California has statewide uniform guidelines for determining child support (see the Tool Box section). The amount set by these guidelines is the minimum required.

Parties and courts may deviate from such guidelines in situations in which application of the guideline would be not be in the best interest of the child(ren) and would lead to an unjust or improper result.

Focus on these questions:

- What do we want for our children (school, activities, clothing, food, internet, etc.)?
- How can we use our income to give them the quality of life we want?
- How can we manage money so it does not cause ongoing arguments between us?

ASSETS

The first thing you need to do is to create a complete list of assets, whether owned jointly or separately. The types of assets often owned by a couple include:

1. Real estate such as houses, condos and land.
2. Contents of the family home—furniture, appliances, equipment, furnishings.
3. Vehicles—automobiles, boats, motorcycles, RV's, etc.
4. Ownership of a company, business or professional practice.
5. Securities—mutual funds, stocks and bonds.
6. Checking, savings and money market accounts.
7. Life insurance policies.
8. Pensions and retirement accounts, IRAs and college savings accounts.
9. Collectibles—family heirlooms, antiques, art work, jewelry, etc.

It's worth taking the time to collect this documentation and place it in a folder or binder. You will need this information to prepare your Schedule of Assets and Debts (see Tool Box section) and make a financial plan.

Often, you can value assets such as stocks, life insurance policies and bank accounts, by looking at current account statements. **Real estate** values can be established through a realtor, a professional appraiser, or (though less accurate and reliable) by using websites that provide estimates of value. You can get values for **collectibles** at little or no expense from antique dealers, art dealers, jewellers, eBay or online searches.

Valuing assets such as a business partnership, professional practice, retirement or pension plan usually require the advice and assistance of a financial professional.

How can I be sure we have complete and accurate financial information?

Good agreements come from sharing complete and accurate information. You and your spouse need to make full and complete disclosure to one another of your finances. If one spouse refuses to do this you may need to seek the help of an attorney to guide you on how to obtain this information.

In California, you and your spouse are required to complete a form called a Declaration of Disclosure, which includes a completed Schedule of Assets and Debts, a completed Income and Expense Declaration, and copies of all tax returns filed by you within the prior two years. These forms list all of your assets and debts, as well as your sources of income and your living expenses. These forms must be signed under oath.

What is community property?

California is a community property state. Unless you have a premarital or post-marital agreement, income earned by either or both spouses through work efforts during marriage belongs equally to each spouse. All assets and debts accumulated during a marriage are presumed to be community property, unless proven otherwise. Determining whether it's a community property asset or debt doesn't depend on whose name is listed. In California, there are laws regarding the division of assets and debts. (see the Tool Box section).

How do we decide how to divide our assets?

Often the division of assets and debts is decided as part of overall negotiations, whether on your own, in mediation, or in discussions with your attorneys. If you are unable to reach an agreement, you can seek a decision from a judge.

What do we do about the contents of the family home?

Sometimes this is easy. You each know what is "yours" and what will stay in the family home. But, if you can't sort this out, then it may be a good idea to start by making a list. This list should include: all furniture, furnishings, electronic equipment, art work, family photographs, linens, appliances, pots and pans, dishes, jewelry and anything else either of you thinks is important.

Sometimes, decisions about who keeps what items are uncomplicated and happen without argument. However, if you are having difficulty making a decision, you might try this:

> - Each of you puts a mark beside an article you want. This helps focus on what is in dispute and what can be agreed upon.
> - Next, exclude items each of you received from your families or as gifts.
> - Work through the disputed items, remembering it's possible to receive money or other assets in exchange for things you give up, such as furniture, appliances, computers, TVs or kitchen items.
> - If you can't resolve everything in one meeting, don't be troubled. Step away, think about how to resolve any disagreements, and meet again at another time

DEBTS

The first thing you need to do is to create a list of all family debts. This may include:

1. Mortgages on the family home and other real estate.
2. Bank or credit union loans for vehicles or otherwise.
3. Credit card debts.
4. Loans from family and friends.
5. Loans against retirement accounts and life insurance policies.

Generally, as with assets, debts held by either or both of you at the time of the divorce are considered **community debt.** For specific information, see the Tool Box section.

Sometimes it can be difficult to work out who is responsible for the actual debt accrued in a relationship. Credit cards are often used for general family expenses such as clothing, food, gas and household items. Allocating debt can become tricky; for example, when the credit card was used to buy a gift for your spouse, or one of you purchased an item despite the other spouse's objections.

If a debt is associated with a specific item, the person who retains the item is usually responsible for the remaining balance. Otherwise, deciding how to divide community debt is part of an overall financial settlement, and is generally divided equally, unless the community debts exceed the community assets, in which case the court will consider the relative financial abilities of the parties.

It is important to agree on a financial settlement that each of you can manage. You don't want a situation in which one of you struggles to keep the debts paid, begins to get behind, and then the creditor contacts the other party. This leads to resentment, conflict and confusion. It can disrupt the plans you made in the settlement agreement and lead to conflict that affects your co-parenting cooperation.

If you and your spouse have a joint debt, even if your divorce decree requires your spouse to make payments after the divorce, the creditor is not bound by the terms of the divorce decree. If your spouse fails to make the debt payments, you can be liable to the creditor for those payments.

TAX ISSUES

It is important to consider the different taxation options available when you separate. You may need to seek tax specialist advice before making a final financial decision.

Your income tax status will change when you separate or divorce, as you are changing from being taxed as a married couple to being taxed as single persons.

You will find that some of the decisions you make will have different tax implications. Claiming "head of household" can affect your tax payments. Health insurance, unless provided by an employer or available through Medi-Cal, also has related tax issues. There may also be tax considerations in how you divide any of your assets or debts.

There are IRS publications dealing with tax issues in divorce If you are selling property or dividing retirement funds or pensions, you may want to consult an accountant (CPA), financial advisor or attorney about any possible tax issues that could arise.

PENSIONS AND RETIREMENT PLANS

Pensions and retirement plans (we will refer to them simply as plans) can be one of the family's most valuable assets. It is important to think about your retirement when thinking about finances during separation or divorce. That's not easy when just managing things day-to-day can be difficult.

We want to help you think about the family's plans. We can't answer all your questions. We can provide some basic information and point you to places where you can learn more. Check out the sources in the Tool Box section.

If accumulated during marriage, these plans are considered community property.

Basic Types of Retirement or Pension Plans
Most workers are eligible for **Social Security.** There are special rules that determine your rights to Social Security benefits of your spouse.

Some people have established an **Individual Retirement Account (IRA)**— regular or Roth—or SEP (for those who are self-employed) or a similar account.

If either of you is employed by a government—local, county, state or federal (including the military)—you are probably a member of a **government sponsored** retirement plan.

Many workers participate in a retirement plan established through their employer such as a **401(k) account.**

Other types of private retirement accounts are sometimes referred to as **defined benefit** or **defined contribution** plans.

Payments from a pension or retirement account are available to an employee according to the specific rules and regulations of the fund. There are also many legal requirements. Each plan is different. You must gather all the available information about each plan that covers you or your spouse.

Some plans are complicated. It can be confusing to figure out what they are worth, the amount of future payments and how they are paid. In this section on Pensions and Retirement Plans you'll find a check-list for the kinds of information you will need. If this seems overwhelming, you may want to consult with a pension expert or family law attorney who can help you understand how your family's plans work.

Rules

Plans are governed by special rules, regulations and laws.

Some of these policies deal with:

- Amount of benefits and how they are paid.
- When they may be paid—at what age.
- To whom they are paid, if the worker is divorced or deceased.
- Whether money can be withdrawn before retirement—and for what purposes.
- Fees and taxes due for early withdrawal of funds.
- Whether you can borrow funds in a retirement account and for what purposes.

What information will you need?

The following is a check-list of basic information you will need to understand any type of plan.

- The name of each plan in which you or your spouse might have benefits.
- Names, addresses and contact details of all employers, through which you or your spouse may have contributed to an employment pension or retirement plan.
- Dates of employment and the names of employers where any pension or retirement account was established for either of you.
- Information about any of the plans in which you or your spouse is participating. You can often obtain a pamphlet or booklet from the employer or plan administrator.
- List of any private or self-employed pension plans, past and present, such as an IRA, SEP or 401(k).
- Contact information for the plan administrator of any of your plans.
- Most recent benefit statements from all plans from the lists above. If you can't locate this information, contact the employer, former employer or plan administrator.
- Benefit statement from the Social Security Administration for each of you. You can easily request this information.

What should you know about your pension or retirement accounts?

The most important information to collect is:

- What type of pension or retirement plan is involved? Is this an individual, company sponsored or government plan?
- When did you or your spouse become eligible to participate in the plan?
- Who is the plan administrator—what office or agency maintains and invests the funds, provides reports, and will disburse payments?
- What is the value of the pension or retirement account? For accounts such as an IRA or 401(k) this information is contained in annual or quarterly reports. For other types of retirement plans, you may need to make a specific request to the plan administrator.

- If the plan or account existed prior to your marriage, what portion of the value accrued during your marriage?
- Are there special rules or regulations concerning a divorced spouse (and remarried spouse)? Often, there are specific rules for such plans.
- What are the plan rules regarding payment of benefits such as: the age when the employee is eligible to receive payments, the amounts to be paid, and the frequency of payments?
- Are there any income tax concerns?
- Are there any survivor benefits? And if so, who might be entitled to the benefits?

You can't proceed properly without this information. Take the time to track it down before you have any discussions about dividing pensions or retirement accounts.

Dealing with pensions under the circumstances of separation can be difficult and confusing. As always, if you have questions, seek professional advice.

How a retirement or pension plan can be divided.

There are a number of ways in which Plans or their value can be allocated. Here are some ideas—they are not the only methods.

For certain plans or accounts, the non-employee spouse establishes a separate account, and the plan administrator transfers funds into this new account. That account will be subject to the same rules and regulations that apply to the employee.

One common method for dividing an IRA involves the receiving spouse opening a new, separate IRA account and transferring funds from the original IRA. This is better than cashing in a portion of the IRA and transferring the money. If you do this, the owner will incur income taxes and possibly penalties on the distribution.

For many retirement accounts, the future benefit payments can be divided with each spouse receiving a portion. The plan administrator pays part of the monthly payment to the non-covered spouse once the covered worker is eligible for retirement benefits.

For Social Security, if you were married for at least 10 years, you may be eligible to receive a payment as soon as the covered person is eligible to receive benefits. See links to the Social Security Administration in the Tool Box section.

How do you make a decision about your Plans?

At the time of divorce, you and your spouse will need to decide what to do with this asset. Even if payments won't begin for many years, you need to determine how to divide the pension or retirement accounts.

In California, pensions and retirement accounts, to the extent accumulated during the marriage, are community property. Unless you and your spouse agree to divide the pension in a different proportion, the community property portion of pensions are allocated equally between both spouses. The following questions may help you in dividing your assets, including your pension benefits.

1. What is the value of each retirement or pension plan?
2. Does one of you have a larger pension?
3. How are the pension and retirement benefits taxed in comparison with other assets?
4. If the asset has appreciated in value over time, what is the value after taking into consideration capital gains taxes?
5. Will the property division make you "house poor"?
6. Is your emotional attachment to certain assets impairing good decision making?
7. Can the party receiving the house afford to refinance the mortgage to remove the other party from liability?
8. Have you considered your long-term financial needs and how the property division impacts such things?
9. Are there family assets, in addition to retirement or pension, that you can use to achieve a fair financial settlement?

Talking about pensions and retirement funds can be hard and stressful work. You may be overwhelmed by the amount of information. If you make a commitment to talk together, you will be able to reach a fair and honest agreement. And, remember, if you are confused, find someone who can explain how retirement plans work to advise you about how your family's retirement funds should be divided.

The glass represents a person's working
life - the total number of years you or
your spouse work before retirement.

Let's assume
your working
life will be 40
years.
This might
include years
after the
divorce or
years worked
before you
were married.

Let's
assume
you and
your spouse
have been
married for
25 years.

The part of the pension or retirement that is
considered community property is
25/40--the years of your marriage divided
by the total working years.

Division of pension and retirement plans are often detailed and complicated.
If you have any questions you should seek the advice of an attorney.

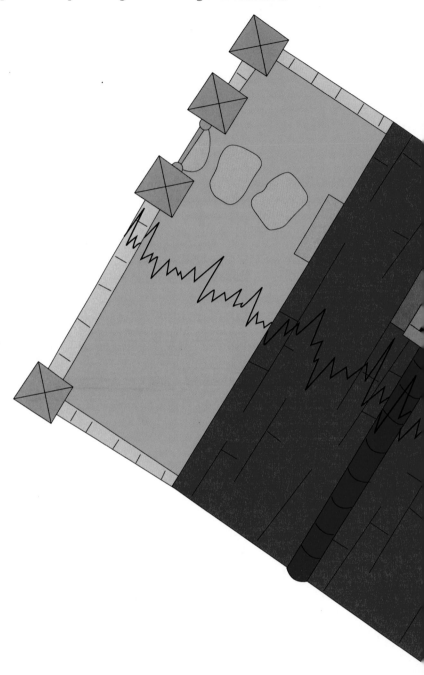

(3)

MARITAL HOME

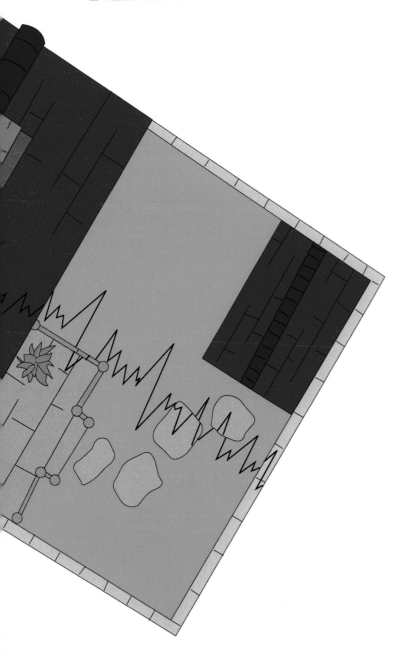

Often the first decision is figuring out who will remain in the family home—whether it's a rental or a house you own. This is a difficult decision because both of you may want to stay in this home; because each of you has an attachment to the home; because it's difficult to pack up and move out; or because you don't know how you can afford two places.

Factors to consider:

1. Can either of you afford to stay there? Or, do both of you need to find a new place to live?
2. For the person who stays, how will you pay for the rent or home mortgage?
3. Is the cost for this place reasonable, or do you need to find a home or rental that is less expensive?
4. How much space will each of you need for yourselves and the children?
5. Is it important for your children to remain in this home because it's close to their school and their friends? Will you be able to stay within the children's school district?

Making the decision:

Although you may feel emotional about staying or leaving, you must be practical and realistic. Before you can decide who will stay in the home, you probably need to figure out whether either of you can afford to remain there. It's possible that your family finances will be stretched too thin.

Use the "kitchen table" guidelines (pages xiv, xv) to help you talk about this decision.

Try this...

1. List the reasons you want to remain in the home.
2. If you had to move, make a list of what you will need in a new home.
3. Review both lists and mark what is essential and what is not.
4. Note what you would give up or trade with your spouse in order to stay in the house.
5. What could you offer your spouse to agree you can stay in the house.
6. If you get caught up in an argument over the family home, go back to this list to remind yourselves what you are aiming for.

VALUING THE FAMILY HOME

If you own a home—whether you keep the home or decide to sell it—you'll need to come up with an idea of its value. It is pretty common for each of you to have different ideas of how much the home is worth. For example: if you want to remain in the home, you may think it has a smaller value; but if you want to sell the house, you may think it is worth more.

It's probably fair to say that neither of you has a completely objective idea about the value of your home. Often, it's a good idea to get a professional valuation from a realtor or an appraiser. Here are some ideas:

1. Agree on a method: valuation from a realtor, professional appraiser, use the recent sales of similar nearby properties. A professional appraiser will charge a fee for this service. There is very little or no cost for the other methods.

2. If you use a realtor, or if you compare your home to recent sales, make sure you rely on at least 3 examples of sales within the past 6 months so you have a range of values to compare. And, make sure the homes you use for comparison are truly similar to yours.

3. If you choose a realtor or professional appraiser, make sure the person is unbiased, has no connection to either of you and is trustworthy and professional. That will prevent disagreements based on the person's qualifications.

CHOICES REGARDING THE FAMILY HOME

There are many options for dealing with the family home. A few are listed below.

Selling the family home

Ashley and Lamar decided they couldn't afford to keep their home. They will sell the property. Each will use money from the sale to buy a smaller place. They want their 3 children to have a comfortable home, near their schools and friends.

Here is what they plan to do:

1. Agree on a value, then determine an asking price.

2. Determine the amount they could receive from the sale of their home, after paying off the mortgage and any selling costs.

3. Sell the home themselves since some neighbors did this successfully. But they will list the property with a realtor if they are unable to sell the home after 90 days.

4. Set a goal of selling the house within 45 days.

5. If the house doesn't sell after 90 days, decide whether to keep the same price, or lower it? Agree on a "bottom line"—the lowest price they would accept.

6. Share the equity (sale price minus mortgage and sales costs) equally. Deal separately with other assets and debts to make sure the overall financial settlement is fair.

7. Figure out whether to make any improvements or repairs before selling the house, and if so, how to pay for those costs. Decide how to promote and advertise your house, including when to schedule showings for buyers, what kind of real estate contract they will use, and whether they need a real estate lawyer to prepare the contract.

One spouse remaining in the home

Lucia and Mateo have talked about what's best for their 3 children, and since Lucia works part-time and has been the children's primary caregiver, they agreed she and the children will remain in the family home. They live in a neighborhood with lots of other children and the kids can walk to school. Mateo will rent an apartment. They now need to decide the value of Mateo's share in the property and how he would receive that amount.

The steps they follow are:
1. The first thing they decided is that any equity in the home should be divided 50/50. They aren't sure how they will do this, and are trying to come up with a plan.

2. They need to know the value of their home in order to determine the equity. Then they can decide how to deal with Mateo's portion.

3. They are considering three options for dividing the equity:
   (i) Cash payment: They need to determine whether they have enough available cash to make this possible.
   (ii) Adjust the division of other family assets and debts: Because they have some savings and a retirement fund, they might be able to make this work.
   (iii) Pay a certain sum at a set time in the future: One option for them is to defer payment until the youngest child graduates from high school or turns 18. Another option is that the money would be due if Lucia remarries or is an equivalent relationship. Payment would also be due if the house is sold.

Signing over the home

For Mary and Jim there is little to discuss. They know there is little equity in their home. They could sell it, but Jim wants to stay and is willing to take on the support and other responsibilities. Mary plans to move to a rental closer to her work. They have agreed that Mary will sign over the home to Jim, and he will arrange with the bank to have Mary's name removed from the mortgage. After they figure out whether there is any equity, Jim will pay Mary her share in monthly installments over 6 months.

Deferring a decision on the home

Portia and Sean have 4 children, 11-year old twins, an 8-year old and a 5-year old. They want the children to stay in their home. It's close to schools and family members. And, it's a great neighborhood for kids. Sean is OK with the plan and will find an apartment where the children can spend time every week. Unless they decide together to sell the house, this plan will work until the youngest child completes high school, if Portia remarries, or is an equivalent relationship.

Some questions they need to consider include:

1. What happens once any of those contingencies has been met?

2. Will the amount due Sean be based on the current value minus the mortgage, or the value at the time he is to be paid? Who gets credit for the reduction in the mortgage balance?

3. Who will be responsible for paying the mortgage loan and other costs of owning the property? Or, will those payments and costs be shared?

4. Since they own the house together, who will pay for repairs and support (such as a new roof, replace a refrigerator, repair a broken door lock or a plumbing blockage)?

5. If they are co-borrowers on the mortgage loan, does Sean need to be concerned about the potential impact of this arrangement on his credit standing?

Negative equity

In some cases, the value of the family home can be less than the amount owed on the mortgage. This is called negative equity (or underwater), and can be a very serious problem. There are a number of options for either holding onto the house or selling the property. Because this can be a tricky situation, it's best to consult a experienced realtor or real estate lawyer.

If you are thinking about refinancing the home in one of your names after the divorce, please speak with a mortgage broker or banker. Mortgage companies have rules about who qualifies. It may be more difficult or easier than you think to refinance in one person's name.

WHEN CHILDREN ARE INVOLVED...
...THE REAL PICTURE

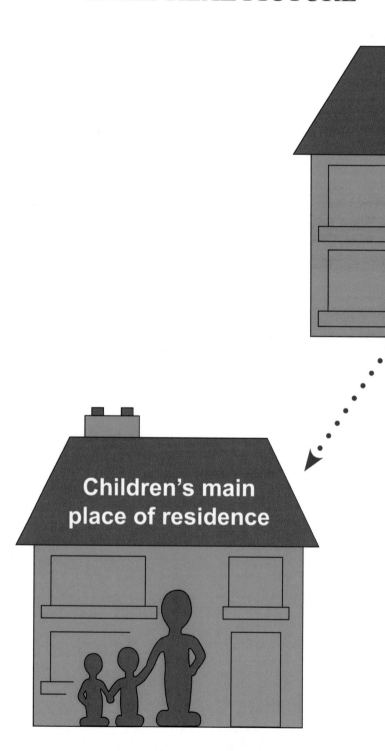

Children's main place of residence

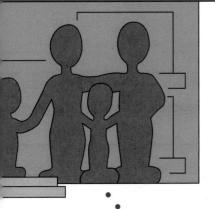

Family
Home

Children's second
place of residence

FAIRNESS

How will you know what is fair? Is it possible to measure fairness—are there criteria you can use? Or is fairness just something you just know in your gut—you know it when you see it?

In divorce negotiations the question of what is fair will always be present. It's there when you think about sharing time with your children; it's there when you talk about finances. What makes it difficult is that fairness is not always something you and your spouse will agree on. And, that's frustrating, but it's normal. It's also possible to come to an agreement that both of you accept as "fair."

One way that couples sometimes end up arguing about fairness is to state, "I have a right." Maybe that's true. And, maybe you need an attorney to fight for your rights. But, before things between you and your spouse become so heated and nasty, maybe you could try to find a fair solution. Here is a suggestion that involves the marital home. The same method works just as well for parenting decisions or any other issue you want to resolve with your spouse.

All good decision making begins with good information. Be sure you have what you need to talk with your spouse and come to an agreement. Then use these facts to help you think clearly.

- Is your current home a place where the children are most comfortable because it's familiar? How long have you lived there? Are the children happy in this home? Is it close to the children's school and friends? Is the home near family or friends who can help if needed? What other factors make this a good place for the children?

- Is the home convenient to where your spouse will live? Will it be easy for the children to transition from one home to another?

- Are you comfortable in the home? Do you have friends in the neighborhood? Do you feel safe there? Is it close to your work and to other places you go frequently (grocery, pharmacy, shopping, religious services, family members)?

- Can you afford it? Is your income from all sources sufficient to pay for the rent (or mortgage), utilities and other expenses? Will you need to give up things you enjoy in order to live in this home (such as meals out, new clothes, entertainment, etc.)?

- Is it the right size--not too small or too large?

- Is it easy to maintain? Will you be able to keep up with repairs and regular support— either yourself or by paying for those services?

- What other reasons are there for remaining in the home?

- Why would you consider moving?

It's impossible to be objective like a computer. It's impossible to rely on facts alone. As we pointed out on page iii, divorce is emotional. Our feelings influence our decisions. If you gather good information, you will be able to think clearly about your decisions, even when your emotions are strong.

Remember:

1. There is never just one right answer. You are unique and your situation is unique. Be willing to consider ideas and options that are different from the ones you started with.

2. If you and your spouse get stuck and aren't making progress, sprinkle some SALT (pages 20, 21) on the conversation. Use the SALT techniques to help you break through the log-jam.

3. It's good to stand up for what you think is right. It's also good to make decisions that leave both of you feeling that the outcome is fair.

WHEN ONE OF YOU CONTINUES TO LIVE IN THE FAMILY HOME

If one of you is staying in the family home and the other is living elsewhere, it is important to agree on some ground rules.

Ground rules can include who provides transportation, where you will meet, how to handle changes in plans, whether your spouse can enter the house to collect or drop off the children. Agreeing on basic rules can make things easier down the line.

Children see the exchange as the most stressful time for them. Children may cry or act out when they are being dropped off or picked up. This is because their parents use these times to argue and fight. And, because there are worries that the children may not have the right clothes, homework, school books, instruments and athletic equipment.

Every transition is stressful. During the transitions, be attentive to the children. Make the transition as easy as possible for them. These times are also stressful for you and your spouse, under the best of circumstances.

Try this...

1. Be on time. Being early or late only increases anxiety and stress.

2. Be prepared. Have all the items that are going with the children (such as clothing, school work, equipment and instruments) packed and located where you or the children can easily grab them. Minimize the stuff children need to take from one residence to the other.

3. Make a calendar of the parenting schedule for the children and post the it in each home.

4. Have family photos, favorite toys, books and other items at each parent's home.

5. NEVER have difficult conversations during the transitions. This is not the time to talk about money, new clothes for the children, whether your spouse is on time, or similar topics. If there are issues to discuss, schedule those conversations for another time.

6. Use the transition to share information about upcoming medical or school appointments, homework assignments, as well as events in which your children will be participating.

7. Be decent. Your tone of voice can send signals to the children about your mood and about the other parent.

(4)

YOUR CHILDREN

What do we do about the kids?
I never wanted this for them!
How will I hand them over to him or her to look after?
What if they need me?
I'm going to be a single parent!
Does he or she understand what they need like I do?
I am worried! I feel guilty!
I love my kids!
I am going to fight for them!
The kids come first..

What do we do about the kids?
How will I wake up in the morning and not see my children?
I won't be able to read to them and tuck them in at night.
Why shouldn't I have the children? I'm just as important to them
as the other parent!
It's not my fault I have to work long hours.
I am going to miss them.
I love my kids!
I need to fight for them!
The kids come first...

TELLING THE CHILDREN

Telling the children about the separation is one of the most difficult things for couples. How and when to talk with them and what you want to say can be a real challenge. Parents are concerned about getting these things right and they worry how they are going to cope when talking to their children.

It is important to tell your children as clearly and honestly as you can. You should think about their ages and what they can understand. Parents cannot ignore the fact that they have to help their child face this huge family change and that adjusting to the changes will take time. It is not possible to shelter children from the effects of separation, but it is possible to find positive ways to help them deal with it.

Key needs for children during separation:

- Clear explanations from their parents about what is happening and when. (They do not need an explanation of why you are separating.)

- Good relationships with both parents during and after separation.

- Parents who can recognize and respond to their needs.

- Parents who can manage their disagreements and find constructive solutions, rather than letting them go on and on.

- Not to have to choose between their parents.

- Make plans for sharing time with your children that are simple and easy to understand and uncomplicated.

- Keep children out of any conflict and parental decision-making.

- Do not use children as messengers.

- Have parents make all arrangements for parental contact.

What children need to hear:

- We are not happy together anymore and have decided to live apart.

- We are still your mom and dad and will take care of you.

- What has happened between us is not your fault.

- The separation is permanent. We will not change our minds.

- Nothing will ever change the fact that we both love you.

- We are still your parents and will decide a future plan for our family. We will tell you the moment we have agreed on what we are going to do.

- We love you and you can talk to us anytime.

How to tell them:

1. As soon as you and your spouse have made the decision to separate, decide when and how to tell your children. If you delay, they will figure it out on their own.

2. You and your spouse should plan what you will say and how you will say it.

3. If at all possible, both parents should tell the children together. If you choose this approach, you must be focused on the children and their needs. If you are unable or unwilling to talk with them together, then agree what each of you will say.

4. Leave aside feelings of anger, blame or guilt you have towards each other. Children do not do well when they are in the middle of parents who are arguing.

5. Children need to hear clearly that you are separating, that you love them, will always be present in their lives, and that it is not their fault.

6. Leave time over the following days to listen and respond to their questions - they will have many. It can take time for children to understand and make sense of what is happening. They may need to go over it many times.

7. Each child will react in different ways. They may cry, withdraw or become angry. Be patient and remember that your children need you now. Being honest with them and available to hear them is hugely helpful to them.

8. If they are upset, let them know it is normal and understandable. Make sure they know that you and your spouse will always be there to take care of them.

Most children say that they would have liked to have known about their parents' separation sooner.

How to support them:

1. Children look to their parents for comfort and support. If they see you being positive, they will feel better themselves. Be positive, but also realistic.

2. Maintain as much continuity and routine as possible. Keep friendships, sports, other activities and school attendance. Carry on with their usual activities. A child who feels secure and positive will cope better with the separation.

3. Keep your child informed about what is happening and answer their questions. NEVER share information about court proceedings with your children or allow them to see any legal documents. It is important for children to know that you are listening to their wishes and feelings. But, remember, you and your spouse are in charge of these decisions. **Do not** ask your children for advice or suggestions.

> **Remember: Never** ask your children to choose between parents. Do not ask your children where they want to live. Very few children are mature enough to make such decisions.

4. Encourage other family members (on both sides of the family) who have good relationships with your children and to remain involved in their lives.

5. Resist the temptation to make up for your child's loss with material things or lack of discipline. Emotional hurt is best healed with care, support and consistency in parenting, not things.

6. Encourage your children to join a peer support program—there may be one at their school. Children find it helpful to meet other children who have had similar experiences. It helps them feel less lonely.

7. Let all significant adults in your childrens' lives know about the separation so that they can help support the children.

Try answering these:

1. When you were together, how did you share the parenting of your children? In what ways were each of you involved in parenting your children?

2. No matter what happened in the past, can you and your spouse make a commitment to work together now for the sake of your children?

3. Are you able to communicate well about your children?

4. Are you able to make decisions together, without constant conflict?

5. Do you have basic respect for your spouse as a parent?

6. Can you allow each other to parent in your own style? Can you agree on essential things such as school and homework, and let go of less important matters?

7. Are you able to work out differences in your parenting styles?

8. Are you aware of and do you value what the other parent has to offer your children?

9. Are you willing to cope with the extra work involved in a shared parenting plan?

PARENTING TOGETHER

Parenting your children will not be the same after separation.

You will both experience the feeling of loss. There is no way this can be avoided, so it is better to acknowledge and deal with this circumstance up front.

There will be many strong and conflicting feelings at this time:
- You may want to hold on to what you have, feeling that any loss of time with the children is like losing your role as a parent or losing your power to help shape their lives. You will probably feel sad about not reading to them at night or being there when they learn to ride a bicycle, or helping them with homework.
- You may feel the other parent does not understand your concerns for the children and thinks that you are getting revenge through them.
- The idea of your children sleeping in a different house can be unbearable.

Everyone in the family feels unsettled, confused and stressed. And, as a result you, your spouse and the children may be on edge. Children feel worried about their future and what might happen, as well as sad and worried about losing time with either parent. Parents have similar feelings of loss and uncertainty.

But, you're the parent! You need to be able to set aside your feelings whenever your children need you. Put your children's needs first.

That doesn't mean you ignore your needs, anxieties and concerns. It just means that you make sure that you are able to care for your children. Then, you can deal with your own needs and emotions.

Children do not want parents other than the ones they have. They love you and want you to look after them. They are resilient and vulnerable. They can cope, but they need your care; they need you to be involved.

Generally, shared parenting can work well for your children. If you and your spouse cannot make this happen without constant bickering, look into a concept known as parallel parenting.

Parent education programs are designed to educate parents about the many issues children face when their family structure changes. The classes focus on how to help children adjust to a divorce or separation, or parents living apart. The classes also provide information to parents about developing co-parenting skills. See the Tool Box for information about parent education classes.

PARENTING PLAN

A parenting plan is that part of your separation or divorce agreement that sets out how you and your spouse will act together as parents for your children. This plan includes important elements such as:

1. Who is responsible for making decisions about your children:
As parents, you are already jointly responsible for making decisions on your children's health, education and welfare. You may decide to retain joint decision-making, or to give one parent responsibility for certain decisions, or even all decisions.

2. Who your children live with:
Children often have a main place of residence with one parent, and time, including overnights, with the other. Some parents share the time equally. There needs to be a clear week-by-week schedule so that everyone knows who is staying with whom and on what day. It can be very helpful to have a clear schedule—perhaps a calendar at both parents' residences— showing the weekly, holiday and vacation arrangements.

3. How will you share holidays and special events?
Start by thinking about what days in the year are special for your family. What holidays are most important? Links to helpful information on creating a plan for holidays can be found in the Tool Box.

This chart illustrates one of many possible ways that parents can share time with their children.

	Monday	Tuesday	Wednesday	Thursday	Friday	Saturday	Sunday
Week 1	P–A	P–B	P–B	P–A	P–A	P–B	P–A
Week 2	P–A	P–A	P–A	P–B	P–A	P–B	P–B
Week 3	P–A	P–B	P–B	P–A	P–A	P–B	P–A
Week 4	P–A	P–A	P–A	P–B	P–A	P–B	P–B

Parent A = P–A

Parent B = P–B

4. Transportation

In order to work out a schedule for spending time with the children, you will need to think carefully about who will pick up and drop them off. Creating a detailed schedule is the best way to make sure there are no hiccups. You and your spouse should agree on a well-defined arrangement for times and locations. Taking time now means fewer conflicts in the future.

You may have been arguing for years and are worried about what the children have seen and heard. You might feel that it is too late. Well, it isn't, and your children will learn that solving problems is possible, no matter how serious the conflict.

It can be an important life lesson to learn that:
- Even when a situation has been bad for a long time, it is possible to turn things around.
- Even when arguments are fierce, it is possible to make peace.
- Even when a problem seems impossible to solve, there is almost always a reasonable way to resolve it.

As you work your way through your divorce and settle into your new life, you will find it easier to settle into this new life.

Try this...

Answer these questions:

1. How much time do you spend with your children when you can give them your full attention?

2. Has your parenting time been affected by the conflict between you and your spouse?

3. How has this conflict with your spouse stopped you from being the parent you want to be?

4. What would you like to change about the way you and your spouse discuss and solve problems?

5. Can you make those changes? What would it take?

6. If you asked your children what they would like to change about you as a parent, what do you think they would say?

How do we make a parenting plan?

NOBODY LOVES YOUR CHILDREN OR KNOWS THEM LIKE YOU DO

You and your spouse know your children best. You know what they need. You know what you can provide. You are the ones who can design a parenting plan that will work.

Research shows that, if parents negotiate their own plan, (1) it is more likely to work, and (2) they tend to stick to it. Try to work out a plan youselves, and if that's too difficult, don't give up. Go to a mediator who can help you negotiate your parenting arrangements.

Here are some ideas of how to do it yourself:

1. Arrange a time when you are both able to sit down and talk for about an hour, without interruptions.

2. Bring a calendar so you can view the weeks, months and year (especially holidays, school vacations and other special events).

3. Bring a notebook so you can keep notes of your discussions (not to keep tabs on each other).

4. Bring photos of your children and put them on the table. If you slip into an argument, look at the photos. Think of what your children would say to you right now. Remind yourselves that your children love you both.

5. Use the template on page 85 as a guide. There are also wonderful resources for separating parents in California. Look in the Tool Box section for links to helpful information.

6. Think about what the children want—and what they need (such as time with each of you, time with their friends, stability in the schedule, etc.). Reading this chapter should be helpful.

Consider the following:

Residence:
- When will they stay with each parent and for how long?
- How will you arrange the transfer between households?
- What will you need in each house for the children (such as special objects like blankets, dolls, cuddle toys; clothing; toys; computer; musical instruments and athletic equipment)?

Holidays:
- How will you organize time during major school vacations—Christmas, Spring, Summer?
- Will you make arrangements so the children can share vacations with each of you?
- How will you share special holidays and events such as Mother's Day, Father's Day, Thanksgiving, Christmas, family birthdays and other days when your family or your spouse's family has celebrations)?
- Will you alternate years for these holidays?
- Can you come together for some time on the day itself?

Financial Support:
- What are the needs of your children per month?   -
- How will you cover the costs for the needs of your children?
- Do you need to create an account for future expenses and needs?
- How will child care be paid for?
- If any of the children are involved in activities such as athletics, music, dance and art, how will you decide about their participation and payment of the costs for lessons, equipment, etc.?

Routine Care:
- Who will oversee the medical/dental needs of the children?
- Who will be responsible for school homework, activities, transportation?
- Who will be responsible for arranging child care?

Authority for Decision Making:
- How will you make decisions about education, medical care,
- religion and other important matters?
- What areas require joint decision making?
- Do you need to make a list of these areas?

Disagreements:
- How will you handle disagreements?
- How will you communicate—in person, email, text, phone?
- How will you make sure you are both on the same page?
- Will you use a mediator when there is a dispute?
- Will you seek assistance from a knowledgeable professional, such as a child specialist or parenting coordinator?

BEING CO-PARENTS

As co-parents, the most important thing you and your spouse can do for your children is to work cooperatively and without constant conflict. There will be disagreements from time to time—this is true for all parents.

Maybe one of you will be late to collect the children or forget that it's your day to have them. Or you asked a family member to watch the kids while you go out on a date and didn't ask the other parent if she/he wanted to be with the children.

At least once, each of you will forget to tell the other parent about a school event, doctor's appointment, play date or dance recital.

And, you may disagree on whether your 12-year old is mature enough to have a cell phone, whether eating certain foods is unhealthy, or how to handle homework.

There will be a time when one of you buys something for the children without consulting the other parent, then expects to be reimbursed for ½ the cost.

Differences between parents are inevitable. How you handle them will determine whether your children will live with bickering, blaming and bitterness. How you handle them will determine whether you build a pattern of working cooperatively or constantly arguing. How you handle these differences will determine whether your children see examples of cooperation or confrontation.

To help address disagreements in the best possible way, use these guidelines:
1. **NEVER** argue with the other parent in front of the children. **HEARING** their parents argue upsets them, makes them anxious, leaves them feeling confused, and causes them to worry about what will happen to them.
2. If you have a problem to discuss, make sure you have privacy and enough time. Unless it's an emergency, make a plan to talk. Don't "ambush" the other parent with your concerns.
3. Be clear with the other parent about your concern and what actions will resolve your concern. It isn't helpful to say, "You don't really care about your children." OR "You aren't a responsible parent." You may feel that way. If you want results, if you want things to be better, then these kinds of phrases don't help. Instead try, "When you miss their games, they get the feeling you don't care about them." OR "Being late is a real problem for them and for me."
4. **NEVER** speak badly about the other parent to the children. They do not want to hear someone they love being criticized. They don't want to take sides.
5. **NEVER** use the children as messengers.
6. Follow the SALT guidelines, see pages 20 and 21.

THROUGH YOUR CHILDREN'S EYES

Children are often the first to realize that things are wrong between their parents. They may not actually know what is happening. They are attuned to even the most subtle changes in the household. You may not think they are aware of what's happening. But, every day, they experience the arguments, the hostile silences and the ups and the downs of your relationship. Long before you ever talk with them about separation and divorce, they will wonder and worry. Many children say that they wished their parents had told them sooner. They want the truth.

When you eventually talk with them, the emotional impact on the children is significant. Children need clear information (based on their ages and ability to absorb and process what you say). Once you tell them, you must support and comfort them in dealing with their reactions to your separation and divorce.

Children need to talk about how they feel. They may feel:

Angry: At Mom and Dad for doing this to them.

Anxious: About everything that's going to happen.

Relieved: That at last they know what is going on. And, maybe the fighting will stop.

Sad: At the losses they face.

Confused: At the explosion of feelings and how they should react.

Grieving: At the loss of their family as they know it.

Guilty: Because they believe it is their fault.

Remember these important guidelines for any parenting arrangements:

- Children will thrive when both parents have an active and consistent role in their lives. (Note: there may be special reasons why one parent has a different role with less or no contact with the children, including a parent's medical or emotional illness or disability, incidents of spousal abuse or child abuse, or if one parent lives a great distance from the children's primary residence.)

- Even when one parent cannot be as actively involved in parenting, children will do well if parents cooperate and work together to resolve problems.

- Active and positive communication provides each parent with information about school events, behavioral or medical concerns and academic issues. Communicating—whether in person, by phone, text or email—allows parents to work cooperatively.

- Children do best when there are consistent rules in both households. When children are very young, these rules should be nearly identical. Older children can cope with differences in the rules at each parent's home.

- Children should be allowed to bring special items from one parent's home to the other. As well, each parent should have the clothing, equipment, musical instruments, supplies and other items the children need.

DIFFERENT STAGES OF CHILDHOOD

How children cope with separation will depend on their age. You and your spouse should develop a plan that addresses the unique needs of each of your children.

INFANT AND TODDLER

I bond with my parents through their care and play.

I need to see each parent regularly.

I need both parents to have the ability to understand what I need and know how to look after me.

I need a regular routine that does not vary from day to day.

I learn to feel safe and secure through a stable daily routine.

I need to be held often, spoken to gently, and caressed.

I need transitions from one house to the other that are easy, not rushed and not stressful.

- The parenting schedule should include regular time with both parents.

- Children benefit from spending time in both houses, but grow anxious if they are away from one parent more than 3 days.

- There should be a stable and consistent routine in both houses for waking, feeding, playing, taking walks, napping and bedtime. This is what they need to feel secure.

- In each household, there should be one person—preferably the parent—who looks after the child.

- If one parent has not been caring for the child on a daily basis, then there should be a transition to a schedule that permits that parent more time with the child. This allows the parent to learn and become comfortable with the baby's routine, and allows the child to adjust to that parent's involvement. As the parent and child become more used to one another and their routine, overnights can be included.

- If both parents have been caring for the child then overnights should be included from the start.

- If you have regular child care that has proven reliable and responsive to the child, it is best to keep the same arrangement.

- Concentrate on your child while you are with them. Be there for them, interact— talk, read and play with them. Don't be distracted or spend time on your mobile phone.

- The baby's routine must be kept consistent in both parents' houses. This is what they need to feel secure.

See the Tool Box: Birth Through Three, A Guide for Parents, Creating Parenting Plans for Young Children

PRE-SCHOOL: AGES 4–5

I want my independence!

I want to choose my clothes and dress myself.

I want to take on some responsbilities like cleaning up my room.

I have learned to say "no."

I am working out what it means to be a girl or boy.

I need time with both my parents to help me do this.

I need lots of reassurance that they love me.

I worry about being abandoned.

I have no concept of time and get anxious when I don't see one parent for a long time.

I want to spend time with my friends, have them come to my house, and go to theirs.

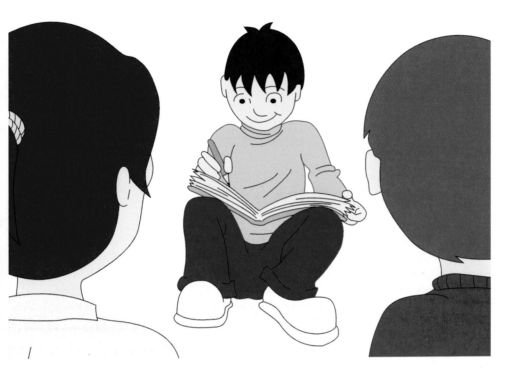

• At this age, children still need a consistent routine at both houses for sleeping, eating, playing and other activities.

• Keep good communication with the other parent; share information about school, the child's friends and activities, their mood and health.

• There are many ways to do this such as email, text and phone. One really useful method is to write down information in a notebook that can be handed back and forth which cuts down the need for long conversations at the hand-over times.

• If you are sharing the parenting, think in terms of 3-4 day blocks when working out the schedule.

• Keep the time-sharing routine consistent.

• Use a calendar to mark the days, so the child can see the schedule.

• If one parent has been the principal care giver, then build up the time away from this parent.

• Both parents should attend school events.

• Concentrate on your child while you are with them. Be attentive, listen and interact.

SCHOOL AGE: 6–12 YEARS OLD

I have friends and my own world of school, activities and play.

I want to learn and get involved in activities, like sports and music.

I want things to be fair.

I can become very angry with the parent who I think has been unfair to me (or with the other parent).

I sometimes worry about the parent I feel is lonely or sad and I may try to make things better between my parents. This is not good for me.

If things aren't going well between my parents, I can withdraw, get stomach aches, have trouble sleeping, or have problems at school.

I need to know that I will have regular time with both my parents.

I want my parents to make sure I can see my friends, be on teams and take music lessons.

- Work hard to keep good communication with each other.

- Take time to organize both homes so the children don't constantly worry about not having the right clothes, books, musical instrument and outfits for school and sports.

- You can be more flexible with time-sharing schedule, as long as the changes are not so frequent that your child is confused and anxious.

- Reassure your children that you are both working to make things fair, and they do not need to worry.

- Reassure them that they can talk to you about anything. And, if there is a problem, you and the other parent will sort it out.

- Help your children keep good consistent friendships.

- Assist your children to choose activities that match their interests and abilities.

- Make sure they have time with their friends.

- Be prepared to provide transportation so the child can participate in activities and be with friends

- Concentrate on your child while you are with them. Be there for them, listen and interact.

ADOLESCENTS: 13–17 YEARS OLD

I want my independence, and if necessary, I will challenge you to get it.

I need to be able to make choices for myself, even if I make mistakes.

I am almost an adult, and I have my own values.

I don't always agree with my parents.

I have my own friends and can make (some of) my own decisions. But, I still need guidance, structure and support from my parents.

I don't always accept it, but I need my parents' advice and I benefit from knowing they are there for me.

I will stop respecting and listening to my parents if they constantly fight.

I don't want to hear about their problems. And, I don't want to carry messages between them.

I love them both.

I need my parents to provide me with some structure and act as a united front.

I need a flexible time schedule so I can spend time with my friends, participate in activities at school and elsewhere, and still be part of my family.

- The parenting schedule needs to be flexible. This requires regular communication between parents so they can keep tabs on the child. At this age, children may try to act more mature than they are.

- Regularly scheduled time is still a good thing, but you need to make it possible for the child to drop in and spend time with you.

- Recognize they will be spending more time with their peers and away from you.

- Attend all school events—teacher conferences, performances, games, and other activities.

- Do not confide in your teenager. Your child is your child, not your friend.

- If there are problems, agree on a united position before you talk to your children. They need their parents to speak with one voice. Inconsistency creates confusion and stress.

- When reasonable, involve children in decisions that affect them.

- Do not put your teenager in the middle of your fights. They may be old enough to have opinions, but they love you both and will not do well being asked to choose sides. The most important rule of co-parenting: keep children out of the middle.

- Concentrate on your children while you are with them. Be there for them, listen and interact.

HELPFUL TIPS

1. Each day brings fresh challenges for any parent. Do not be too hard on yourself. Your children will come through this if you make an effort to do your best.

2. You and your spouse should be focused on creating a good working parenting relationship for your children.

3. Have reasonable expectations for yourself, the other parent and your children. The shift to a two-household family requires patience, persistence and planning.

4. Minimize your children's loss. You can help them adjust to their new lives by focusing on what you can maintain—family relationships, routines, schools, friends, activities. **You cannot erase what's happened or make things perfect.**

5. Reassure your children they are loved and are not the cause of your separation.

6. Help them connect with the other parent, as much as reasonably possible. Don't force the issue. Never criticize the other parent to your children.

7. Create a working partnership - one that is based on a good parenting agreement.
    - How would you talk to them, and how do you want them to talk to you?
    - How would you approach them with a problem?

8. Find effective ways to communicate with the other parent. It can be helpful to arrange regular "meetings" with the other parent. If possible, and if you and your spouse can talk without blaming and bitterness, schedule periodic meetings to talk about the children.
    a) Arrange a neutral venue.
    b) Agree on an agenda.
    c) Agree not to bring up the past.
    d) Set a reasonable time limit.
    e) Do not discuss difficult issues during the hand-over.

Hint: Use a notebook to keep notes about information the other parent needs to know. If texts or e-mails result in arguments, find other more effective ways to communicate.

9. Separate your couple relationship from being parents. As time goes by, you will each become less important to the other as intimate friends. What you share is the parenting of your children. Focus on working successfully with your ex-spouse as your children's parent.

10. Talk with your children. Ask them what they need from their parents. The feelings that overwhelm you at the time of separation can blind you to the needs of your children. Think about your children's hopes and fears. What are their child-like worries? Do they need help adjusting to the new situation? How do your children feel about each of their parents? Listening to your children's concerns can help you focus on their needs.

11. Think about what this new situation will require from you. If your children are old enough, can they help with chores so you have more time and energy for them?

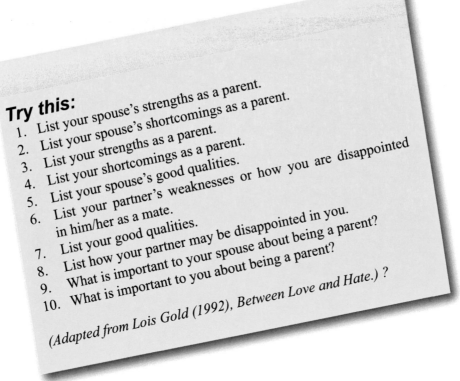

Try this:
1. List your spouse's strengths as a parent.
2. List your spouse's shortcomings as a parent.
3. List your strengths as a parent.
4. List your shortcomings as a parent.
5. List your spouse's good qualities.
6. List your partner's weaknesses or how you are disappointed in him/her as a mate.
7. List your good qualities.
8. List how your partner may be disappointed in you.
9. What is important to your spouse about being a parent?
10. What is important to you about being a parent?

(Adapted from Lois Gold (1992), Between Love and Hate.) ?

Look at your responses. Do you see similarities in your parenting styles? How can you use those in working together? What are the differences in your parenting styles? Can you use these differences without being in conflict with each other?

JUST BE PARENTS

Couples who manage to separate their relationship as a couple from their role as parents tend to handle their separation or divorce more positively. These couples put the needs of their children ahead of their own feelings about one another. They talk with one another, as parents, not as spouses.

If at all possible, find a way to work with the other parent. It's not always possible. Sometimes the other parent doesn't want to cooperate, may be abusive, addicted to drugs or alcohol, or otherwise unsuitable as a partner in parenting your children.

Remember, the bond between children and parents continues despite divorce. Your children will almost always want some connection and contact with the other parent. If that's true, and if it's possible, help your children maintain that connection. Don't allow your bitterness, anger or frustration about the divorce to become a barrier to cooperative parenting.

Children want to love both parents freely and without complication. They want to be the subjects of their own lives and not the objects of their parents' arguments. They will not take sides or stop loving one of you simply because the other parent demands it. Asking your children to take sides is unfair and wrong. And, it will backfire on you.

Children want to attend events like birthdays and holidays, without worrying whether their parents can be in the same building together. They never, ever want to have to choose between you.

Children deserve the best of each of you. After the divorce, you can still raise your children to be happy and secure. It is a matter of learning to be parents in a new way.

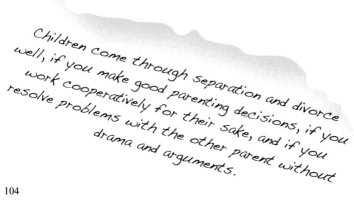

Children come through separation and divorce well, if you make good parenting decisions, if you work cooperatively for their sake, and if you resolve problems with the other parent without drama and arguments.

NEW PARTNERS

The arrival of a new partner can be highly controversial for parents, particularly if it is someone that one of you met prior to the separation. If a new partner creates serious conflict between you and your spouse, it is worth using the services of a mediator or family therapist to help you discuss and address how you handle this issue, so you can work together for the sake of your children.

Your children will never want to replace either of you as parents. They will not see a new partner as a potential parent. They can develop good relationships with the new partner, if a few simple agreements are observed. While this may be a very difficult thing to accept, it is healthier for your children to get along with this new person.

If children are left to figure out what is going on by themselves, they can soon become distressed and confused. Unless you tell them, they don't know who this person is, and how they are supposed to act around the new partner. Children need to understand what's happening. Their anxiety can cause additional stress for both parents. Conflicts can erupt and parenting arrangements that had been working can fall apart. In the end, it's the children who struggle and suffer.

Try this:

1. Agree that for a substantial period of time—at least six months—neither of you will introduce new partners to your children. This helps the children get used to the separation without the additional challenge of seeing their parents with other partners, and without the stress of figuring out what role that partner will have in their lives.

2. Agree that you will accept your spouse's right to a private life.

3. Be prepared to talk about the impact on your children of new people coming into your lives.

4. If you want this new partner to meet your children, talk first to the other parent. The chances are that children will get along with this new person if they know the other parent is at least aware of the new situation.

5. Do not tell the other parent the night before the planned introduction or on the door step when you pick up the children for a visit. Doing this will create tremendous tension for the other parent and your children.

6. Leave time for more than one conversation with your spouse about the new partner, and keep the discussion focused on the needs of your children.

7. If one of you plans to move in with a new partner, arrange to meet to discuss any necessary changes to the parenting plan, including what role that new partner will have - if any - in parenting the children.

IT IS NEVER TOO LATE

Take time to look ahead

What do you want your children to say about their parents when they are young adults?

" My mom and dad split up when I was young and they..."

How do you want that sentence to end?

How you behave as parents affects your children, especially after a divorce. They are deeply affected by what they experience through us. You are their model for being a parent.

Children learn by watching and listening. What do you want them to learn? If you and your former spouse can cooperate—at least work together without intense conflict—you will help your children deal with the divorce. You can teach them—not just by words—but by how you and your spouse behave.

But, if you allow your children to be in the middle of arguments, they learn that problems lead to arguments, and arguments mean the problem isn't solved. Do you want them to learn that disagreeing with someone means calling the other person names and shouting? Or, do you want them to see that their parents can work together? Do you want them to learn that it's OK to disrespect someone and that dishonesty is acceptable. Or, do you want them to see that you and your spouse can disagree without resorting to name-calling and blaming?

When children see their parents fighting without solving problems, they end up feeling responsible for the conflict or feeling it's their job to find a solution. The divorce was not their fault. They aren't responsible for fixing things. You and your spouse can help your children by showing them that you two can work out your differences, you can solve problems—without bringing the children into the situation.

> ***Experiences*** "I see my dad all the time. He takes me to baseball and basketball games and we get along okay. Mom has to do the school stuff so she gets it from me. I'm sorry I do that, but I can't help it. I love her really."
> Matthew 16 (read more real life experiences go to Chapter 6)

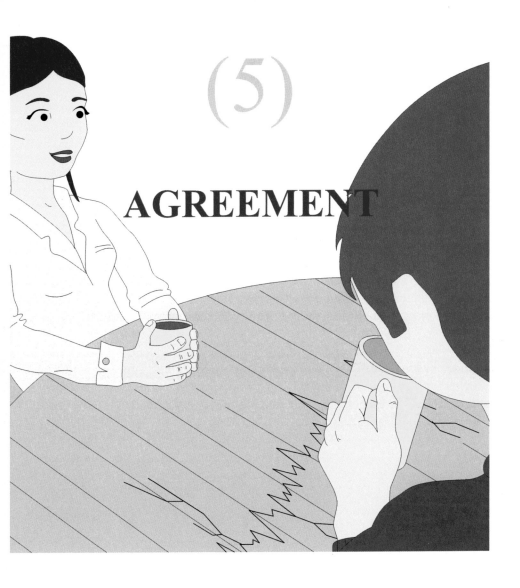

(5)

AGREEMENT

The agreement that you negotiate will be the foundation and road map for the next phase of your lives. Where and how you live as separate adults and how you raise your children will be profoundly affected by the terms of the agreement.

Agreements work best if you and your spouse are honest with each other, talk openly and often (even if you ask a mediator to help you), and recognize that it can't be all "take" and no "give." It might feel great to win an argument or "get one over on the other" when fighting about things like money or parenting. However, there is no doubt that in any agreement you will each need the other to deal fairly with you. Just as your spouse is looking for you to be reasonable and fair on one issue, you will be looking for the same attitude from her/him on another topic.

PREPARING AN AGREEMENT

Once you both reach the stage where you recognize that separation and divorce is inevitable, you need to turn your attention to the details of finances and parenting. Whether you work out these arrangements yourself, with a mediator, or with the assistance of attorneys you will need an agreement (often referred to as a Marital Settlement Agreement - MSA). The following section describes what such an MSA would contain.

The MSA is a formal document signed by both of you and attached to and incorporated into the judgment, which (along with additional forms) is submitted to the court for filing. The divorce is finalized once the judgment has been entered. The Agreement reflects how you and your spouse see the future. It's a contract and will be part of a court order - the divorce judgment. But, most importantly, the Agreement must be realistic and practical and based on your family's needs and resources.

If either of you has hired an attorney, then you can ask one of the lawyers to write the Settlement Agreement. When couples work through mediation, but are not assisted by an attorney, the mediator may write up a Settlement Agreement. If you wish, you may then review the proposed agreement with an attorney.

If you and your spouse have negotiated your own agreement, it is important to consider having the Settlement Agreement drawn up by an attorney—especially if there are complicated arrangements about parenting, finances, property and pensions.

The following is an outline of the main issues you would be covering and the information needed.

As we have said repeatedly, every family is unique and every divorce is unique. That means that every MSA is unique.

It's not OK to use the sample language we provide without considering whether your situation is exactly the same as the one we are using as a sample.

You should carefully consider what goes into the MSA. The terms of the MSA have serious legal consequences. If you have ANY questions, consult an attorney.

> **Note: You can find (and download) a sample MSA from the California Courts website. See the Tool Box section for the link.**

Written clauses may look like this...

1. We, Jim and Mary, were married on May 15, 1998 in Los Angeles, California.

2. The date of separation of the parties is January 1, 2016.

3. We have three minor children named Betty, born on May 3, 2002, Anne, born on July 6, 2005, and John, born on September 8, 2010.

4. Irreconcilable differences have led to the irremediable breakdown of the marriage, and there is no possibility of reconciliation.

5. Except as otherwise provided in this agreement, the purpose of this agreement is to make a final and complete settlement of all rights and obligations between the parties, including all property rights and, if applicable, all rights and obligations concerning child custody and visitation, child support, and spousal support.

Note: the sample language provided is for illustration purposes only. Consult an attorney to be sure your Settlement Agreement is properly written and is complete and accurate.

Children / Main issues to discuss and include:

1. Are you clear how decisions concerning the children will be made? Will you do this jointly, or will one parent have sole responsibility for some or all decisions? If you plan to share some or all decisions, how will you deal with any conflicts? For example, what if you disagree about participation in an after-school activity, or about who should pay for equipment or instruments? Will you both attend parent-teacher meetings or arrange separate meetings? Another important issue can be whether the children have access to and how they use digital devices and television.

2. Have you prepared a detailed parenting schedule that you both understand? Have you planned for transportation?

3. Will the schedule allow the children to continue their activities and spend time with friends? Have you dealt with holidays, school vacations and family events?

4. Have you and your partner agreed how to handle unexpected situations that could affect the schedule? Can you agree to be flexible, or is it best to keep to a schedule, no matter what? Who will care for a child who is ill and can't go to school or day-care? What happens if one of you needs to work extra hours? Can you two discuss and resolve the possible need for flexibility in the schedule or other parenting matters as they arise? How will you communicate about the needs of your children?

5. Will the children be able to contact the other parent on their own? If so, are there any restrictions on when, for how long, and by what methods?

6. How will you share information about schedules for school events and other activities such as athletic games, lessons, and recitals? Relying on your children to tell the other parent almost never works out well. Can you each make a commitment to inform the other parent? Can you arrange for the school to send notices to both parents? Can you organize a shared online calendar?

For further information about parenting schedules, parenting plans, and related resources, please see the Tool Box section.

School Vacations, Summer Holidays and other Special Events.

How will you share time with your children during these periods?
We agree that we will share time with our children as follows:
- School summer vacation: (timetable)
- Mid-term breaks: (timetable)
- Federal and state holidays, and other dates when the children are not attending school: (timetable)
- Christmas/winter break: (timetable)

Taking Vacations with Children
What arrangements would you like to make for taking vacations with the children? By what point in the year will you need to have decided on vacation dates?
Is it acceptable for each of you to take the children out of the state or out of the country for vacations? Will you agree on who will keep the children's passports? Will you agree (good way to phrase this).

Christmas, New Years, and Religious Holidays
A clear plan for each holiday should be negotiated well in advance.
Sometimes parents agree:
- To alternate holidays that are important to your family.
- To each have the children for a portion of the day.
- To spend time with the children together.
- To share holiday and school vacation times.

Child Care and Babysitting
Each of you will need a babysitter from time to time. Do you:
- Give the other parent the opportunity to be with the children, remembering that the other parent is entitled to say no on their nights/weekends off?
- Agree a shortlist of babysitters you are both happy with that you can use?
- Each make your own arrangements?

Birthdays and Other Special Days

The children will be with each of us on alternating years for their birthdays. Mom will have the children in odd-numbered years; Dad will have the children in even-numbered years. The children will be with each parent for that parent's birthday, with Mom for Mother's Day and with Dad for Father's Day.

Education/School Meetings

1. We are satisfied with the present arrangements for the children's education. We agree to review these plans during the summer after each school year and decide whether to keep the same plan or make changes.
2. We agree to keep each other fully informed of educational progress of Betty, Anne and John by exchanging copies of their report(s) and by attending parent/teacher meetings, either together or separately, as appropriate. If the school district policies permit, we will request that the schools provide separate copies of all reports and notices.

Communication

1. We agree that, while our children are spending time with either one of us, they may have reasonable contact with the other parent. Depending on the children's ages, they will be able to initate the contact.
2. We agree that the absent parent may contact the children by phone/text/skype.

Passports and Travel

1. We understand that in order for our children to obtain passports in their own right, we need to give our consent as their parents. We therefore agree to give whatever consent is necessary when required. The parent requesting the issuance of the passport will pay the costs and fees. Once issued, the passports will be in the care of (either Mom or Dad).
2. We both consent to the other parent taking Betty, Anne and John out of the State at any time the children are scheduled to be with that parent, provided the other parent is given a complete travel itinerary.

Note: The sample language provided is for illustration purposes only. Consult an attorney to be sure your MSA is properly written and is complete and accurate.

FINANCE

Main issues to discuss:

1. Child support and other expenses for your children.

• California has adopted guidelines for calculating child support (see Tool Box section for a link to the guidelines and forms).

• Costs for the children (other than the regular day-to-day expenses) such as: school fees, costs for activities such as sports and music, uniforms, tuition for school, summer camp/day care.

2. Spousal support.

If there is the possibility of support for one spouse (alimony), make sure you have all the budget information you need to decide on an amount and the duration. In the Tool Box section you will find a link to California law regarding spousal support.

3. Miscellaneous support provisions.

• Have you agreed how any changes in child support or spousal support will be decided? By law, child support can always be modified (by agreement or by the court) for one of many reasons. See the Tool Box section for more information.

Depending on how you structure spousal support payments, they can also be modified.

• Sometimes, if finances permit, parents agree to provide life insurance in an amount that will cover child support or spousal support payments if the person paying should die.

• Consider various tax provisions that may affect your decisions. Some of these items include: dependent exemption deduction, child tax credit, head of household filing status. See links in the Tool Box to the IRS website for further information.

• Who will provide and pay for health insurance for the children as well as co-pays, deductibles and non-covered expenses such as vision and dental.

In California, the cost of such health insurance is included in the child support calculations. Co-pays, deductibles and non-covered expenses are typically shared equally by both parents, unless agreed otherwise.

> **Note: Making smart decisions about all of these financial matters requires a careful review of all information.**
>
> **The language in the MSA must be accurate and clear. If you have any questions about these provisions, consult an attorney.**

Written clauses may look like this...

Child Support and Spousal Support

Jim is employed by OGX Stationers, Main St, as an accounts manager. The children are included on medical insurance available through Jim's employer and the premium is deducted from his salary.

Mary is self-employed part-time as a physical therapist.

Having looked at our financial needs and the needs of our children, and based on our parenting plan where the children spend 70% of the time with Mary, we have agreed that Jim will pay to Mary the sum of $2,200 each month, divided as follows: $400 to Mary as spousal support and $600 for each child until the first to occur of the following events: child dies, Mary dies and Jim assumes custody, the child is emancipated, or the child reaches the age of 18 (except that an unemancipated 18-year-old unmarried child, who is a full-time high school student and is not self-supporting, shall be entitled to continued support until the completion of the 12th grade or attaining the age of 19, whichever first occurs). Spousal support will continue until the earliest of: the death of either of us, Mary's remarriage, or further order of court.

Payments will be made on the first and fifteenth of each month into Mary's bank account at Main Street Bank and Trust.

We will share equally all unusual child-related expenses such as school fees, athletic uniforms, band instruments, summer camp and day care.

Jim will maintain the life insurance policy on his life, until all financial obligations for child support and spousal support are satisfied and Mary will pay the premiums on that policy. Jim will name Mary as beneficiary and the children as secondary beneficiaries.

Note: The sample language provided is for illustration purposes only. Consult an attorney to be sure your MSA is properly written and is complete and accurate.

Review of Financial Arrangements
We will evaluate the amount for child support annually after filing our income tax returns and when there are unusual, unexpected expenses for the children.

Income Tax
We will file separate tax returns beginning the year of our divorce. For the prior year, we will file joint tax returns. Jim will be responsible for any additional taxes due and we will share equally any refunds.

Assets and Debts
1. We own real property at 8642 Bungalow Lane; vehicles, bank accounts, Mary's IRA, Jim's employee pension, household furniture and furnishings, a collection of antique plates, a motor scooter, and Mary's jewelry.

Mary will live in the family home and pay all expenses including the mortgage loan, property taxes and insurance pursuant to the terms in this MSA. A legal description of the property is attached as Exhibit A.

Mary will retain her jewelry, her vehicle, the collection of antique plates, the IRA account, furniture and furnishings in the family home (except for those given by Jim's parents), and one-half the amounts in the checking and savings accounts.

Jim will retain his vehicle, his pension, the motor scooter, the furniture given by his parents, and one-half the amounts in the checking and savings accounts.

2. We have the following debts: a mortgage loan on our home, Jim's car loan, Mary's VISA card (last 4 numbers), Jim's Discover card (last 4 numbers).

Mary will pay the balance on the credit card in her name. Jim will pay the car loan and the balance on the credit card in his name.

We agree that each of us will be responsible for any personal debts incurred by us from the date of this Agreement and will not hold the other person liable.

Note: The sample language provided is for illustration purposes only. Consult an attorney to be sure your MSA is properly written and is complete and accurate.

Alternative language for medical costs and health insurance...

We have agreed to share equally the costs of all deductibles and other unreimbursed medical expenses for the children.

We will discuss in advance and agree on non-emergency medical, dental, vision, orthodonture and other treatment for the children.

Jim will provide and pay for medical insurance for the children and provide details to Mary.

Mary will obtain and pay premiums for her medical insurance.

Note: The sample language provided is for illustration purposes only. Consult an attorney to be sure your MSA is properly written and is complete and accurate.

Alternative language for dealing with the family home...

The family home at 8642 Bungalow Lane, Chicago, IL is held in our joint names. We value this property at $300,000. There is an outstanding mortgage of $180,000 with Main Street Bank and Trust.

Mary will continue to live in the family home until the youngest of our children reaches the age of 18 or completes high school, whichever occurs later. At that time we will sell the home and divide the net proceeds (including repayment to the person who paid for any significant non-routine support costs and improvements) equally.

Mary will pay the monthly mortgage payments, insurance premiums, real estate taxes and all utilities. Mary will also be responsible for and pay the costs of routine support. For any major repairs, replacement of equipment and improvements, we will discuss what is necessary, and then share equally the cost for the work we have agreed is needed.

OR

We have decided to sell the family home. We have agreed to put it on the market with the Smith Real Estate Company at an asking price of $300,000. We will divide the net proceeds, 60% to Mary and 40% to Jim.

OR

Jim agrees to transfer his entire interest in the family home to Mary. Mary will pay Jim the sum of $45,000 within ninety (90) days of the date of the divorce. Mary will assume and pay the outstanding mortgage and will indemnify and hold Jim harmless against any liability with respect to these payments.

Note: Because the MSA is filed with the court and can be viewed by the public, you may not want to include all these details in the document. They appear in this sample to give you some ideas for your own MSA.

Alternate language for dividing all personal property...

Mary will retain as her separate property her jewelry, all furniture in the living room, dining room and bedroom, furniture in the children's rooms, all appliances, furniture given to her by her parents, the upright piano, the desktop computer and printer, the Toyota automobile; and will be solely responsible for any debt associated with and secured by such property.

Jim will retain as his separate property furniture given to him by his family, the sofa and chair in the den, the Sears riding mower, the Vespa motor scooter, his athletic equipment and the Subaru automobile; and will be solely responsible for any debt associated with and secured by such property. He will remove these items no later than October 25, 2018.

OR

We have agreed to divide our personal property in accordance with the attached list. *(Note: this must be a detailed list indicating who retains each item)*

Note: The sample language provided is for illustration purposes only. Consult an attorney to be sure your MSA is properly written and is complete and accurate.

Written clauses may look like this...
Life Insurance

Jim will keep in force the life insurance policy on his life until all financial obligations for child support and spousal support are satisfied and Mary will pay the premiums on that policy. Jim will name Mary as beneficiary and the children as secondary beneficiaries.

Mary agrees to keep in force and pay the premiums on the life insurance policy on her life, naming the children as the beneficiaries (with Jim as trustee if they are minors).

Jim and Mary each have life insurance coverage available through their employers so long as they remain employed. Mary and Jim retain the right to name the beneficiary on their respective employer-provided policies.

Note: Deciding about life insurance requires careful consideration. If either of you has life insurance coverage, you may want to seek advice from an attorney about how to handle those policies.

Pensions and Retirement Plans

In chapter 2, **Finances,** the key issues for dealing with pensions was set out. Remember there are detailed laws governing pensions in general, and specific rules and policies for each pension and retirement plan. Any agreement you make must be consistent with these laws, rules and policies.

The division of pension and retirement plans may require a Qualified Domestic Relations Order **(QDRO).** There are different forms of this order for every plan. They are detailed and often very complicated. You will need the help of an attorney to be sure the document is accurate and complete, and that it meets all the requirements of the plan. Once it is approved by the plan administrator, the QDRO is presented to the judge for her/his signature.

Sample language for dealing with retirement funds or pension accounts...

1. Mary will be entitled to a share of Jim's retirement benefits in the XYZ Retirement Plan when and as he is eligible to receive those payments. The amount payable to Mary will be a fraction the numerator being the number of years of Jim's employment with XYZ during their marriage and the denominator being the number of years of Jim's eligible employment. We will consult with an attorney familiar with QDROs to complete this part of our divorce.

OR

2. Jim agrees that Mary will be entitled to receive forty percent (40%) of his retirement benefits when and as they are payable according to the terms of the XYZ Retirement Plan. Mary will also be entitled to any death benefits allowed by this Plan.

3. Jim has an IRA account with Jones Investments. Mary will open an IRA account in her own name, and thereafter, Jim will authorize the transfer of the entire balance from his IRA account to Mary's IRA account.

Note: The sample language provided is for illustration purposes only. Consult an attorney to be sure your MSA is properly written and is complete and accurate.

WILLS AND INHERITANCE

A Will is a formal written document that determines what will happen to the deceased person's property (called the estate).

If there is no Will, then the laws of California will determine how the estate will be divided. These laws may give the surviving spouse and/or children automatic rights to a share in the estate of the deceased person.

It is important for you to make a Will because that is the only way to be sure that your wishes will be carried out. A Will can ensure that good arrangements are made for your dependents and that your property is distributed in the way you would like after you die.

Good questions to ask...

1. Does either of us have a Will, and if so, what does it provide for the children and the other spouse?

2. Do we want to change any of the terms of our Wills?

3. What provisions should each of us make for our children?

4. If I need to appoint a guardian while my children are minors to take care of any property left to them, who is a trustworthy person to make sure the terms of my Will are carried through?

5. Should we make an agreement about our Wills as part of our divorce; if so, what terms and items should be included?

6. Do I have all the information I need to make good decisions about this?

7. Do I need more information? Would it make sense to ask the mediator or a financial advisor? Would it be a good idea to seek advice from an attorney?

What happens after we reach an agreement?

Once you and your spouse have talked about all the issues and questions and have reached a complete consensus, you have a couple options:

1. Each of you will meet with attorney of your choosing to review the MSA; make sure your agreement meets all the legal requirements, and that you haven't overlooked or misstated anything. The attorney will also make sure you have all the required forms (such as Child Custody and Visitation Attachment, a current Income and Expense Declaration, Guideline Child Support Calculation, etc.). California doesn't require a hearing. The attorney will prepare any other papers necessary for processing of the divorce and file them with the Court.

OR

2. You can do all these things on your own. It's called acting Pro Per - meaning on your own behalf. If you are confident that your agreement is complete and accurate, you may be able to complete much of the divorce paperwork yourself, but you will probably still want advice from a lawyer. If the divorce is contested, it would be a good idea to consult with a lawyer.

Try this...

Before you sign the Settlement Agreement, ask yourself:
- Can I live with this Settlement Agreement—not just accept the terms, but can I make this work?
- Is this fair enough for both of us and our children?
- Can we be parents for our children the way we want to?
- Can I accept that the Settlement Agreement may not be 100% perfect, and realize it is good, fair and practical?
- Is it complete; have we covered everything?
- Will this work for all of us in the future? How will we review and revise the Agreement if things change in the future?

After you sign:
- How do I move on?
- How do I make the best use of the arrangements for me and my family?
- How do I make the most of my life?

LOOKING AHEAD TO THE FUTURE

Once your Settlement Agreement is completed and signed, it is time to look to the future. Did everything go your way in the separation/divorce? Probably not. But isn't that life? From now on, how each of you lives out the terms of the Settlement Agreement will determine success in your life and for your family.

It may be that your future is not quite as you had imagined it would be. You may not have wanted your marriage to end. You may not want to be single again or to handle so much on your own.

The plan you made may be imperfect. If there are problems, and you and your spouse deal with them in a responsible and honest manner, then you will be able to solve them together.

From now on, the choice of how you live your life is in your hands.

ACCEPTANCE

The loss of a loving relationship brings confusion, anxiety, and loss. One writer, trying to make sense of her own divorce, refers to this period as "crazy time." (Abigail Trafford, Crazy Time) Feeling unsettled, anxious and even a bit fearful are normal parts of every separation and divorce. Negotiating a separation settlement while you are feeling bitter, fearful and anxious can seem overwhelming at times.

However, regrets of the past will eventually be eclipsed by hope for the future. You will move ahead, learning to live with new responsibilities and appreciate new opportunities. Reaching this point can take weeks or months. Some days will be a breeze and others will be more difficult. But, things will improve. There will come a time when you accept your new situation, having grieved the losses, and you just move on with your life.

Try this...

1. After your divorce, do something that will help you feel more positive about the future. It can be as simple as listening to music you enjoy, phoning or visiting a friend, cooking a special meal, or exercising.
2. Take some time to think about all that has happened. It's all too easy to get busy with your life, with your children, and not give yourself time to consider all that you have learned.
3. If you feel yourself getting down, phone a close friend or someone in your family; maybe plan something positive (see #1 above).
4. Make a list of things you would like to do in life that you have not yet managed to do, and make a plan to start on one of them.

If you feel that you are really struggling, seek help from someone whose advice you trust, such as your best friend, a close family member, your clergy person, physician or a counselor.

What kind of person do you want to be?

Someone who never forgets or someone who learns to be happy again?

How long do you want to hold onto the bitter taste of the past?

When do you want to enjoy the sweet taste of the future?

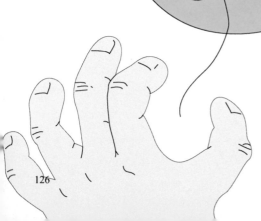

"In forgiveness there is a recognition that nothing we do to punish the other person will heal us.... A choice to forgive is a choice to heal yourself."

– Between Love and Hate, Lois Gold

FORGIVENESS

Some of you may decide to skip this section. For you, the idea of forgiving your former spouse for hurts, slights, and failures is unthinkable. The sadness and pain of a broken marriage, particularly when caused by infidelity or abuse, is too strong.

For those who are ready, forgiveness can be a powerful experience.

Remember forgiveness can only be given freely.

With the ability to forgive comes the feeling of freedom and hope for your future. You take away the other person's power over your life, and you change your own life for the better. You take back your sense of self and stop living through your reaction to someone else. Forgiveness is a process of letting go and looking to the future.

Forgiveness doesn't mean you agree that what happened was okay. Forgiveness comes from understanding how you have been hurt by what has happened, and then finding a way to let go. When you can forgive someone, you release yourself from holding onto the bitterness and disappointment the experiences have caused. The starting point for forgiving is to want to do so and to realize that it may take a long time.

These questions might help you decide if you're ready to forgive:
- What would it mean for you to forgive the other person?
- What would you find hard to forgive?
- How would your life be better if you were able to forgive the other person?
- How do you feel now about how you were treated by the other person?
- What if you could put these feelings aside and not let them bother you?
- Could you imagine being able to separate the person from their actions?
- How would you have liked the other person to have acted instead?
- Can you recognize something good in the other person?
- What do you think they might say about you?
- Could there be anything you did that they might find difficult to forgive?
- What would both your lives be like if you could both forgive?

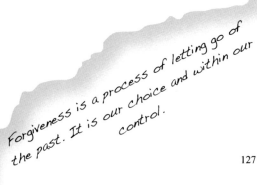

Forgiveness is a process of letting go of the past. It is our choice and within our control.

MAKING IT WORK

Your divorce, like so much in life, is a work in progress. If you have planned well and been able to cooperate with your ex in making parenting and financial agreements, then most of the time, things will work out well. It will not be perfect. When there are problems, just realize you can fix them in the same way you made the original agreements—talking with your former spouse and using positive communication skills presented earlier in this book. For those parts that aren't working as you had hoped, you can decide whether to modify the plans and if so in what ways. It's up to you to decide what you can live with and what needs to change.

You have the chance to make a good life for yourself, and it is in your hands to make it work. Some days will be harder than others, but your new life will slowly settle into its own patterns.

Divorce professionals (mediators, lawyers, counselors and judges) encourage parents to continue talking and cooperating. The greatest source of emotional distress for children is conflict between their parents. The following guidelines will help you stay on course.

If you are parenting with your ex-spouse, remember:
1. If arguments happen, do not talk about them in front of the children.
2. Make the transitions as easy as possible for the children—and for yourselves.
3. Arrange to meet to discuss problems before they become serious.
4. Carefully plan family celebrations, so you do not have any misunderstandings about who is to attend.
5. Do not allow resentment to build up, leading to arguments.
6. Remember, at this point, you are at the end of one part of your life and at the start of a new part.

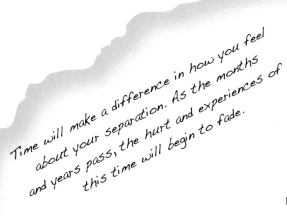

Time will make a difference in how you feel about your separation. As the months and years pass, the hurt and experiences of this time will begin to fade.

LOST DREAMS

Staying Put

Telling the parents

GETTING OVER
THE GUILT

Money, Money, Money

NEW
PARTNERS

Telling the Siblings

Moving On

FEELING INDEPENDANT

(6)

EXPERIENCES

The following short stories are based on conversations with people who have gone through separation and divorce, and about their feelings and experiences. We have changed the names of those involved as well as certain details, to protect people's identities. Some of the stories show both sides of the same relationship.

WHAT KIDS SAY

TELLING THE CHILDREN

Legal Battling

The arguments never stop

LOST DREAMS
A wife's experience

So, this woman with a little boy in a stroller came up to me in the street. "He's your husband's", she said. I stared at her. She said it again, "He's your husband's and he is three years old." I still couldn't believe what I was hearing. I looked at the little boy in the buggy... he looked like my daughter. This was her half brother.... My world came crashing in.

That was six months ago. My husband moved out. He is living in an apartment somewhere. I don't know if he is seeing her or not but I don't care anymore. My life is in tatters. He gives us money, me and the girls, but I can hardly face him when he comes to the door.

I smile and stay calm... for my girls... they still love him so I have to be strong. How can I hate him, love him, not care about him and stay calm all at the same time? Those moments on the doorstep waving my girls...our girls...off. It breaks my heart. They love him but he left them. I know he says he just left me but, to them, he is gone.

I know that I will start to get over this sometime. This feeling of anger and betrayal... but what about the shattering of my dreams? We were a family, we were going to grow old together. We loved each other.... We had just moved to a new house for goodness sake!

All the time he had another child. How do you account for that? This man I thought I knew, taking my future away so casually.

When I think of the future I dare to hope. I dare to hope that I will find someone and I will be happy again. For the moment, I love my girls and they love their mom and dad. So, I need to stay calm, smile and carry on....

LOST DREAMS
A husband's experience

Here I am with four children and I don't live with any of them! I'm not sure how it happened. One minute I was part of a family and was enjoying an affair. I know it was wrong but it just happened like that. Then my son was born and I was so happy. I had my three beautiful girls and now I have a son.

It was all a bit crazy, keeping it a secret from my wife, but these things happen. I know I hurt her tremendously. I hate thinking about that. She looks so sad... and I did that to her. Well, maybe we were not that happy anyway. That's probably why I had the affair.

I do love my children. They are so clever and great fun. I see my girls at the weekend and I pop in during the week to say hello. It is hard to go back to my home like that but I try and keep calm and happy for the girls. They love their mom and I want them to. She is there for them every day. I can't be anymore.

The bit that hurts the most is the fact that they think I left them too. I have tried to explain but they are too young to understand. Their faces on the day I moved out were something I will never forget.

If could turn back time, what would I do? I don't know. If I hadn't met my son's mother I wouldn't have my boy..... But the pain I have caused my family is hard to think about.

I know that I am a good dad and that is what I can do well. I will be there for my kids and I'll try and work the rest out as I go.

STAYING PUT
A husband's view

It was my wife who decided that we should separate. She said that she was not able to live in this dead marriage anymore. She had given us long enough and it was over. Dead marriage? I was surprised... shocked. I know things weren't great but we got on okay. There were no real disagreements, no big arguments. She says we fell out of love. I thought that we still cared enough about each other to make it work.

The thing that really makes me angry is that she says it is over and I have to move out.... Apparently it is me who loses my home, me who sleeps in a crummy apartment and me who stops living with my children.

Since when did her well-being become more important than me being a dad? I will not move out under any circumstances!

We have three beautiful kids and I am going to be here for them. I don't want to be a weekend father or a McDonald's dad. I am their dad, that means 24/7—homework, bedtimes and breakfasts... nothing less.

Why does the man always have to move out? I could live with her quite happily. I like my home. I love my kids. I care about her. All she loses is a husband she doesn't want, but I lose everything. No way! I have worked too hard for all of this. I will fight this. She can't make me do it and the kids need me here.

STAYING PUT
A wife's view

I don't know how much more I can take of this. We live in the same house but can't sit in the same room as each other. We love the same children but can't agree on how to be their parents. We share the same marriage but have nothing to say to each other.

Can he not see what it is doing to us? What it is doing to the kids and me? He is so stubborn. It is all about him and his needs. Well, he has to go. He just has to. What does he think we can do?

I am the one who looks after the kids. I am home every day after work to do home-work and feed them. He is never home until 8.00 p.m. He is out in the morning. Don't get me wrong, he has always worked hard. He is an excellent provider. But he and I have nothing in common.

All this business about being a dad. The kids know he's their dad. I won't stop him seeing them. They love him. In fact, things will be better when he moves out. He has to be the one that moves. I can't afford to. I only work part time and if I am not here for the kids then who will be? Is he going to get a baby sitter?

It makes no sense. Deep down he knows the marriage is over. We both do. I am so sorry and sad about it all, but I can't make it better anymore.

THE ARGUMENTS NEVER STOP
The regrets of a couple

We have been separated for three years and we still can't be in the same room. We just make each other so angry.

We met twelve years ago. We got on like a house on fire and fell in love. When we got married we were so happy. We adored each other and had such fun. Our two kids were born, a boy and a girl, and our family was complete. It is hard to know how things started to change.

There were little problems, small fights. We hurt each other. Things got worse. Our home stopped being a calm place... it felt tense all the time. The children stayed outside playing with their friends or went to their room. They knew the signs. First icy silence, then a sharp word. The atmosphere in the house would change as we traded insults. We would scream and shout, not caring who heard. I can feel it now, the anger, the hurt. I feel sick thinking about some of the things he said to me.

Our friends didn't really know what was going on but they stopped coming around. He went out with his friends and I went out with mine. They were great. I used to talk about him all the time. My friends said I should stick up for myself. His friends said the same to him. There was one friend who tried to stop us.

I remember what he said. He asked us if we were going to keep on like this. Point scoring and judging each other. He said that we were about to lose ourselves to this fight. We didn't listen.

We even argued in mediation. We were trying to sort out our money. He didn't seem to get the fact that I didn't have enough to support the girls. He kept saying over and over I should work more hours, take in a renter or cut down our spending. I used to shout back at him that he didn't care about his family. The mediator talked to us about how we were lightning rods each other. The anger that we felt was so strong it clouded out everything else.

I remember what she said. She asked us something. She asked us if we thought our fighting might be a way of avoiding the sadness of our parting. If we kept fighting, we would not have to face the reality of being alone... apart.

We ignored the question, left mediation and headed for court. Our fight was made for court. We fought every step of the way. Our attorneys gave us what we needed: the feeling that each of us was right. We each felt justified in holding our ground.

I do remember one thing my attorney said, though. He asked me if all this fighting was costing me my family life. He talked about how we should remember that this would all be over one day and we would still be parents of the same children.

We didn't listen and sat in the courtroom glaring at each other. The judge took the responsibility of making the decisions away from us. We could blame him, if we didn't get what we wanted. The judge asked us if we loved our children. We said yes. Then he said that he didn't love them, in fact he had never met them, and yet we wanted him to decide about their future. He wondered why we couldn't do this ourselves, despite professing our parental love for them.

We ignored him and carried on.

I look back and wonder about all of this. Did we have times when we could have stopped?

The people who could see what was happening had tried to make us see that we could have chosen how we split up. We could have remembered what we used to appreciate in each other and remember to be parents.

We found it too easy to blame each other and not own up to our part in the fight. When you get that angry you pretend that you want it all to stop when, in fact, you want the other to change and yourself to win. What a waste of time, what a waste of money and what a waste of a family.

When we left the court on the final day of our divorce hearing, I thought I would be so happy. But I was just exhausted. And the funny thing was that the next day he was coming to pick up the children. We had torn each other apart and now we had to get on with our lives, still parenting our children.

And it's not like the written agreement we got was much different. It was almost the same as what we would have reached in mediation and what our lawyers were prepared to settle on. We could have saved a lot of time and money, but we had to have our fight.

I see him sitting in the car, building up the courage to knock on the door. He hates coming to the home he once lived in. The kids look at me nervously. They think there are going to be more hot words, more tension. I look out. The kids have their school play this Friday. They are more worried about how we will behave than whether they remember their lines or not.

So, here we are. Him sitting in the car and me waiting at the door with the kids. Maybe time will help. If I knew then what the fighting would do to us, how long it would go on for and how much hurt it would cause, I would have done things differently.

TELLING THE FAMILY
– THE CHILDREN
A father's story

I don't think either of us will ever forget telling our three children we were separating. My wife and I talked for months about how to tell them.

We had decided to separate after years of trying to make it work. It was just over and we both knew it. We had no idea if our kids had guessed anything was wrong. Our middle girl had asked a few things but we didn't know what to say to her. We had decided to tell them together. The books said that this was best and we were determined to get this right. However, the thought of it was almost too much to bear.

We sat them down one evening after dinner. We had agreed that my wife would start, but as she opened her mouth the tears started to fall. My daughter looked at her. "You're splitting up, aren't you?" she said. There was silence. The children looked at us. We looked at each other and then at them. "Yes, we are," I said.

I was amazed that they knew so much. The little one was shocked but the other two said that they had been expecting this for some time. We told them we loved them and that we were still their mom and dad and nothing would change that. They asked us where they would live. We said we were not sure but we hoped to keep the family home for them.

My son was angry. He was angry that we had not told him sooner. He had been worrying. He has a friend whose parents fight all the time. They had just lost their house. We tried to assure him that this would not happen to us.

Our youngest asked, "If you're not fighting any more why don't you stay together?" That was a tricky one to answer. My wife told her that we just couldn't live together and that, now we had decided not to, it had helped us to stop fighting. I don't think the little one understood but that's all we could say.

Over the weeks the kids asked us lots of questions. Some we could answer but others we couldn't. We were as honest as we could be. They were angry at us, upset that their lives were changing and worried a lot of the time.

Part of our plan at that time was to take the kids out now and again, one at a time, so we could talk. I took my son out bowling and to football. My wife took our daughter into town and the little one had trips to the ocean and park. Sometimes we talked about the future, but a lot of the time we talked about other things.

138

My wife and I hurt each other a lot over the years. There were days when we couldn't look at each other, but somehow we managed to work together as parents. Telling the kids was hard. Being there for them was awkward when they asked those difficult questions but they came through the separation alright.

Our children still have their family. It is a separated family, but they have us and each other.

We don't have all the answers for them but when they look back at that time I think they can say, "When mom and dad split up they did the best they could to be good parents... and they were."

TELLING THE FAMILY
– THE PARENTS
A woman and her mother

My parents were very upset when we separated. They said to me that we should stay together for the kids, that marriage was for life and we were giving up too easily. I kept saying to them that they didn't understand. They didn't know what was going on.

After that they never phoned the house. They stopped talking to my husband and were strange with me. I eventually had enough. I went round to their house one Sunday and asked them what was going on. My dad said nothing but Mom was upset.

She said that they didn't know what to do. The day I had arrived to their house and blurted out the news she had been shocked. She liked my husband and didn't want to lose him as a son-in-law. She thought that it might pass and we would change our minds. She said she just wanted me to be happy. I remember her looking at me and asking "What about the kids? We love them. They're our grandchildren." I said to her that they would always be their grandchildren and they missed her. Then we cried and talked for a long time.

My husband and I went to mediation. We told our parents that we were negotiating a plan and when we were organized we would tell them what we were going to do. We asked them to be there for the kids. To take them out and give them some fun while we tried to work out our lives. We also asked them to support us both, if they could.

It was hard, really hard, but we got there. When we had our agreement sorted we arranged to go together to my parents and then his. We sat down and told them that the house would be sold and we were going to have two separate places. We said it was time to put the past behind us and try to start new lives. We thanked them for supporting our family and asked them to do three things:

1. To love and support the children, and not to say anything bad about either of us to them.
2. To respect that this had been hard on us both and that we needed help from our moms and dads to move on.
3. To keep in touch with the other person, if they wished.

They liked the fact that we asked for help and the three things gave them something they knew they could do. I meet my own in-laws now and again.

At first it was a bit strained. Now we can chat away about the kids and the weather. It was worth thinking about them. It helped having them on both our sides.

TELLING THE SIBLINGS
When it goes wrong

When I told my sister she said, "Well, anyone who wants to leave you is nuts! He is quite clearly out of his mind." She phoned my brother immediately and told him he couldn't play golf with my husband anymore because he was a scumbag.

So that was that, the battle lines were drawn, whether I liked it or not, and war was declared. I actually quite liked it, to be honest. I could go to my sister's and talk about my husband as much as I wanted and she was ready to believe everything I said. My brother had been friends with my husband for years. In fact, that is how we met. Now he wouldn't give him the time of day. It is funny how others feel they have to take sides on your behalf.

It all got out of hand when my brother told my husband that he had to find another pub to drink in. "Nobody wants to drink with a cheater," he shouted. There was a shoving match. Nobody was hurt but it was bad enough. I was glad. I was glad that my brother had stood up for me. I wanted my husband to feel bad about what he had done. It was what he deserved.

It carried on like this until my daughter's birthday. We were having lunch at the house when the argument happened. My sister told my husband what she thought of him. He told her she was an interfering old hag. Neither knew that our daughter was listening. My daughter ran out the house crying and was missing for three hours. I was frantic. My husband was worried sick. That was when I grew up.

I realized that getting my family to fight for me, like we were still kids, was not the way to live. My children were in the middle. I was stressed out. The fight was getting bigger and bigger and soon it would engulf us all.

I sat down with my brother and sister. I reminded my brother that he had been friends with my husband since childhood and maybe things had to change, but not like this. I thanked them for caring enough about me to stick up for me, but now I was ready to build bridges for the sake of my kids and the family. I told them I needed their support.

It took a long time to sort things out. My ex-husband and I are now divorced and can talk to each other alright. The golf games are back on. I don't think it is quite the same, but they get along. My sister takes my kids out with her two and has agreed with them not to talk about the divorce. She spoils them, as all good aunts should, and they enjoy themselves.

My ex-husband's family were never as angry as my own. I see them from time to time and they come to the kids' birthdays. I do it for the children and, as time has gone on, it has got easier. To start with we didn't know what to say to each other so we stuck to safe subjects. Now we are more relaxed. Life moves on.

NEW PARTNERS
Ex-wife's new relationship

My ex-wife and I got divorced three years ago. She is living in the family home with our two kids and I have a house quite nearby. She bought me out of the family home and so I bought this one. It all worked out fine and I have the kids to stay regularly.

I had said that I never wanted anyone else to stay in the family home with my kids. My wife had laughed and told me that there was no way she would ever want a relationship again. I suppose time changes a lot of things.

I heard about John from the kids. They had gone to the zoo with their mom and her friend. That was fine, but, after hearing about John a few times, I noticed that the kids stopped talking about him. "That's good," I thought. "He has obviously not lasted long." I was wrong.

The children were a bit awkward when I asked them about their mom. They didn't like to talk about their other home anymore. I couldn't decide what was wrong... and then I got the phone call. It was my ex-wife. She wanted to meet up to discuss something with me.

My ex told me she had met someone, John, and that it was serious. She wanted to introduce him to me before she told the children that he was her new partner. I told her that I thought they had already guessed and that she should have told me sooner. I was hurt and angry... and I wasn't sure why. We both knew this would happen to one of us sooner or later. Maybe I was annoyed it wasn't me!

I met John and actually quite liked him. He said he cared about the kids but wouldn't get in my way as their dad. I told him that he was damn right... he wouldn't. We laughed and it was very awkward. The kids got on with him and they were a lot more relaxed once they knew I was okay with it. I made sure I seemed okay, but it took a lot of getting used to.

Six months later, John moved into my old family home. I remember the day as if it was yesterday. I felt sick with bitterness. Another man with his feet under my table. Living in the house I fixed up. Sitting at the breakfast table and getting my kids out to school. My ex did talk to me about it. We agreed new parenting rules and John sticks to them. I don't want him punishing my kids or criticizing them... that's my job. We had a few arguments and in the end we just agreed to try and get along for the sake of the kids.

It will be a while before I feel alright about this. Don't get me wrong, getting a divorce was the right thing and I want my ex to be happy. I just don't want to feel as if I have lost everything else.

GETTING OVER THE GUILT
A husband reflects

The first five months of the separation were just awful. I felt so guilty about how the whole thing had happened. It really got to me and brought me down. My wife and I didn't want to hurt each other, but we did. Our children were stuck in the middle and then I left.

No matter how I felt, I had to go to work every day. I have my own business and I had to get up in the morning and function. My mind was a confused mess. I would stare at things for hours. Work reports that normally would take me half an hour stayed on my desk unfinished. Co-workers who relied on me had to fend for themselves.

I would start to eat and then stop, walk into my office and then back out again... and all the time I had this dreadful feeling of guilt over the separation. I don't even know how the feeling started, but I really felt to blame.

Eventually my accountant of all people asked to meet me. He gave it to me straight. The business was beginning to suffer and he was worried about me. He told me that he had a brother who had gone through a split and he recognized the signs. He suggested I go to my physician. Actually he told me to go! I did and she referred me to a therapist.

Things began to get better. I did a lot of talking, not something I had done before, and slowly the guilt began to lift. I started eating, work became an interesting challenge again and life began to make sense to me. I started to rebuild my world day by day.

I underestimated what I would feel when my wife and I separated. I thought I would be okay. I think there is a difference between feeling guilty but not letting it get to you and becoming totally consumed by the feeling. I nearly went under.

It is natural to have all sorts of feelings at a time like separation. It is a crisis and it would be strange if you didn't struggle. I know that now. I would tell anyone like me to ask for help. It makes a difference and you will start to recover.

FEELING INDEPENDENT
A woman finds her feet, two years on...

When my marriage finished, I felt lost. My husband packed up and left and there I was on my own. We had been together for 15 years and a lot of those had been good. I collapsed in an emotional heap. I didn't know how to be single!

My lawyer suggested that I work towards a complete feeling of independence. He said it would help me if I handled my own affairs, so I sorted out my own bank accounts and bills. It was a bit daunting at first but I began to enjoy managing my own life.

I could have relied on my lawyer to sort out the separation but he told me that this would not help me in the long run. He insisted that I keep my own notes and make my own decisions. He was right. I followed his advice and it has worked.

We finally agreed on our divorce this month and I felt confident about going into court. We have a good agreement and I think we managed to be fair to each other. I didn't get everything I wanted but, then, neither did my husband, so I suppose that counts as fair.

Anyway, I walked out of court knowing that I was okay on my own. I could take charge of my life and had all my bills, money and accounts in order. I liked that.

LEGAL BATTLING
Managing to communicate, eighteen months on...

The lawyers got involved and we were told not to talk to each other. There was a lot of mistrust and it just got worse and worse. We were both afraid that whatever we said would be used against us. We had no communication at all in the end.

I couldn't believe that it had come to this. We had been married for twelve years, had three children and a business together and now we couldn't even ask one another to pass the milk without a courtroom drama. Every time I talked to my lawyers they told me to stay strong and not to give in. I had to be careful not to be taken in by false promises from the other side. I am sure he was being told the same. It was all so tough and hard nosed. We had no idea how to act around each other when we were with the kids.

For the whole duration of the divorce proceedings, life was unbearable. He accused me of ripping him off; I accused him of deserting his children. We were so bitter. The anger would consume us as we fought it all out. And all the time we couldn't talk, really talk, like we used to.

Then the battle was over, the papers were signed and all was settled. Almost immediately, things calmed down. We still had the hurt but the battle was gone. Things are becoming increasingly calmer and we are actually almost friends again.

MONEY, MONEY, MONEY
How mediation can help sort out money

Mary

We started going to mediation to work out all our finances. I couldn't manage on the money he was giving me and I knew he needed to give me more. We have three kids and a mortgage. I work part time so my income goes out almost as soon as it comes in.

Jim

I don't know where Mary thinks I am going to get this extra money from. My wages are the same as when we lived under the one roof, and we didn't have enough then. This mediation is going to have to show her that you can't get blood out of a stone.

Mary

I sat down and filled in my budget sheet. My God, I can't believe what we spend on the children. The bills are no better. I know we have a summer vacation and try and get away for a few days in the winter, but we need the break. At least Jim will see that I am not blowing his money!

Jim

My attorney says that I don't have to pay Mary what she is asking. He says she will have to cope with what she gets. I need to pay for somewhere to live and have a life as well. This budget sheet shows how much I need. Wait until she sees the real cost of living apart.

After the mediation session

Mary

Well, that was not what I was expecting. When the mediator added all our numbers together and we saw the joint cost of everything, I got a shock. I had never thought of it like that. The two houses and the children's costs coming out of the one pot of money. I know Jim and I earn good money, but when you see it added together and then put it beside our joint expenses it doesn't look nearly enough.

Jim

That was the first time I saw all of the costs written down like that. I can see that we need to tighten our belts, but if I give less to Mary for the kids they will have to stop their sports, and I don't want that. I never thought of sorting out the money this way. If Mary and I can sit down and agree on some mutual savings maybe we can look at the support differently. Whether we like it or not, we are still in this together.

MOVING ON

Jane, 47

"I never thought I would get through this, but I have. It's about 18 months after my husband and I parted, and I have started to feel my personality change. I feel more positive and full of energy. I have started to think of new things I could do and life doesn't seem so full of worry and confusion. I think the most important thing for me was the fact that I had friends and that I could talk to them. I sort of talked myself out of my depression and loneliness... and you do feel alone when you separate. I quite like that feeling now. My independence is something I am proud of. For a long time I was part of a couple and then, when that stopped, I felt as if my right arm had been taken off. I had to start all over again... but I did!"

Alan, 65

"My divorce was ten years ago. I have a new partner, my kids are grown up and life goes on. I look back and almost can't remember what we fought about. We couldn't agree on anything and we ended up in court. It was expensive and painful, but it was all so long ago now. Our daughter got married last year. What a great day that was! We were so proud of her and she looked beautiful. My ex-wife actually hugged me and said that we had at least got one thing right. Our kids went through a hard time, but they came out the other side and live good lives now. We got over the fighting and started to live again. As each year has passed, the divorce has faded and the future has become my reality. It is possible to move on."

Aidan, 37

"I met a woman last week. She liked me and I thought I had a chance with her. Then I remembered that I would have to tell her about my three kids, the mortgages, support payments and the weekend visitation times... no nice weekends away! If I met this girl last year I would have given up, annoyed at my wife sitting in our house with my kids. Now, I will give it a go. She seems lovely and, you'd never know, maybe she has kids too..."

Anna, 53

"My divorce papers arrived today. Twelve pages that ends fifteen years of marriage. I thought I would cry but I didn't. I felt a sort of relief when I saw the envelope, which surprised me. I think I am ready to move on. My ex-husband and I have both found this hard. When we got married we didn't expect this to happen, but, now it has, I am ready to get on with it. I am looking ahead with interest at what the future holds. I couldn't have said that six months ago. I hope I meet someone but, even if I don't, I know I can be happy. I am well and so are the children, and that is what counts."

MOVING ON – THE CHILDREN

Kate, 25

"My dad left my mom when I was twelve. He got remarried really quickly and my mom never forgave him. When he phoned the house, my mom would get me to speak to him. She would stand behind me and tell me to say that he was a cheater and that he didn't love me. She cried a lot and blamed my dad for everything.

My dad used to take me out but then he stopped. He would come to the house and my mom would shout at him. She would scream that he never gave us enough money, she was going to take him to court and that he was a lying cheating idiot! She hated him for what he had done to us.

I didn't see my dad again until I was nineteen. I know he had done the wrong thing but I missed him. It might sound funny but I cannot forgive my mom for what she did. She told me things that were not true and tried to stop me loving him. I nearly did, but as I grew up I began to understand more about life. What went on between them should never have been taken out on me."

John, 14

"My parents were so worried about telling us that they were splitting up that they didn't ever manage to say it out loud until months after we knew anyway. It would have been a lot better if they had told us earlier. My six-year-old sister used to ask me all the time and I didn't know what to say. I was only nine myself. We knew things were wrong and worried all the time about what might happen.

They told us eventually and then things felt easier. We could ask questions and talk about the future. Mom said that we were still going to be a family and, although they were going to live apart, we would still spend lots of time together. I wasn't quite sure how that would work but I could see she was trying to be positive.

That was five years ago now and we are still a family. Even my dad's new girlfriend sort of fits in. If I had one piece of advice to parents it would be to tell your children clearly as soon as you can. They will only worry if you don't. Let your kids ask questions over and over. That is their way of working it out... and remember that we want you both to be happy, regardless of what you have done."

WHAT KIDS SAY

Kate, 15

"I found out that they were separating when I heard my mom shouting at my dad over the phone. It was awful. I was really upset and I didn't know what to say...."

Bobby, 9

"I didn't really know what was going to happen. I knew things were bad but I didn't know what was going to happen next. My dad moved out of the house. I asked my mom and she started crying. My grandmother was there so I asked her and she told me that my mom and dad were splitting up. She told me the truth. I love her for that."

Susan, 10

"My dad told us. He just said it while he was driving along. He said, 'I am not going to live with your mom anymore. It's for the best. We will stop fighting then.' And that was that. My little brothers started crying and I just said, 'Oh'. He dropped us at the door and went."

Billie, 14

"I would have liked to have known more about what was going on. It would have helped if they had sat down and talked to us. We wouldn't have worried then."

Carla, 11

"I wouldn't want to make the decisions. It would be the same as taking sides and I couldn't do that. I just want to know what is going to happen and that they are going to decide for me."

Colin, 13

"It's better now he has left. They don't fight anymore and the house is calmer. I still worry about if he is alright, but it is better."

Ellen, 14

"I worried that my mom would get a new boyfriend and my dad would find someone else, but they have said that they won't. Maybe they will, I don't know. I just want them to be Mom and Dad."

Johnny, 13

"Some people don't like being separated... I didn't like it when my mom and dad told me they were doing this, but I had to get used to it. People can't live together if they don't like each other. That makes sense to me. So, I am okay with it."

Emma, 5

"They shout at each other all the time. We are moving to another house when they separate. That's just what happens, I suppose. At least the shouting will stop."

Sophie, 9

"I see my dad on Saturdays. I worry that he will get sad if I am too busy to see him, so I am always ready. He is always pleased to see me and that makes me happy."

Dan, 12

"My mom was very sad when my dad left. She cried a lot but then she started getting better. I think she is great the way she coped with it all. I think I love her more now."

Zoe, 15

"Mom and Dad have tried really hard to be friends so we can all be happy. I think it is hard for them but they sort of manage to do it. I think it is cool. They are cool. Both of them."

Amy, 10

"Since my dad left I have got closer to him. He tells me he misses me and we talk about everything. He asks me lots of questions about my life and he has time to listen. He didn't used to, so I like it now."

Matthew, 16

"I really argue with my mom and things aren't the best, but then she has a lot to deal with. Mom and Dad split three years ago. I see my dad all the time. He takes me to matches and we get along okay. Mom has to do the school stuff so she gets it from me. I'm sorry I do that, but I can't help it. I love her really."

David, 13

"I would have been happier to see them both all the time but that is not possible. I spend half my time with each of them. It is a bit of a hassle, but I like seeing them."

TOOL BOX

This section provides details and links to a number of websites, that can provide you with specific information on many issues relating to being separated or getting divorced. These links were current as of the date of publication. Please be aware they may change.

Also, state and federal laws and regulations change from time-to-time. We will provide updated information on our companion website, www.divorcebookcalifornia.com

TOOL BOX RESOURCES
California

Divorce in California -
Links to general information about divorce in California and to California divorce forms.

California Divorce Laws
https://leginfo.legislature.ca.gov/faces/codesTOCSelected.xhtml?tocCode=FAM

Information on divorce and separation from the California Courts
http://www.courts.ca.gov/selfhelp-divorce.htm

Information on divorce and separation in California from Law Help CA
http://lawhelpca.org/issues/families-and-kids

A range of general information about divorce and divorce resources
https://www.divorcesource.com/

Helpful (brief) articles on all aspects of divorce
https://www.liveabout.com/divorce-4145430

Basic divorce information (sponsored)
https://www.divorcenet.com/states/california

Family forms from the California Courts
http://www.courts.ca.gov/8218.htm

Programs available for self-represented individuals
http://www.courts.ca.gov/documents/proper.pdf

References to professionals who help people in divorce

California State Bar-certified lawyer referral services organized by county in California
http://www.calbar.ca.gov/Public/LawyerReferralServicesLRS.aspx

Mediation - General information and locating a mediator
https://www.mediate.com/

California Superior Court Custody Mediation
http://www.courts.ca.gov/1189.htm

Court-based facilitators for self-help
http://www.courts.ca.gov/selfhelp-facilitators.htm

Collaborative Divorce
http://www.collaborativedivorce.net/what-is-collaborative-divorce/

Divorce Financial Planning
https://www.divorceandfinance.org/page/DivorceFP
https://institutedfa.com/divorce-information/

Forensic Accounting
https://insights.itsovereasy.com/family-law-how-forensic-accountants-help-you-during-a-divorce

Divorce Coaching
https://www.americanbar.org/groups/dispute_resolution/resources/DisputeResolutionProcesses/divorce_coaching/

Parenting coordination
https://www.apa.org/monitor/jan05/niche.aspx
https://www.ourfamilywizard.com/blog/five-reasons-work-parenting-coordinator

Support groups
Groups led by mental health professionals

https://www.psychologytoday.com/us/groups?search=california

Parents without partners
https://www.parentswithoutpartners.org/default.aspx

Rainbows (for children)

https://rainbows.org/services/divorce-support

Psychological information

https://www.apa.org/topics/divorce/

Information on domestic abuse

http://www.courts.ca.gov/selfhelp-domesticviolence.htm
https://1800victims.org/crime-type/domestic-violence/
http://www.lapdonline.org/get_informed/content_basic_view/8893

PARENTING

Parenting Resources
http://www.courts.ca.gov/16473.htm

Basic parenting plan
http://www.courts.ca.gov/16432.htm
http://www.courts.ca.gov/16473.htm

Help with communication between parents after divorce
coParenter - https://coparenter.com/
Our Family Wizard - https://www.ourfamilywizard.com/

Our Children First and similar classes (required for divorcing parents with minor children, depending on County)
http://www.courts.ca.gov/selfhelp-familycourtservices.htm

Orientation to Family Court Mediation and Child Custody Recommending Counseling (if in a recommending county)
https://www.youtube.com/watch?v=wJOcjP5RikQ

Parenting classes
http://www.courts.ca.gov/16473.htm

DIVORCE FINANCES

Divorce financial planning - Excellent basic resource for understanding finances and divorce:
Divorce Financial Planning Guide: Expanded Third Printing Kindle Edition by William Morris

Deciding about your family's home:
https://www.amazon.com/Divorcing-House-Understanding-Could-Should-Keep/dp/1936268973

Helpful software to guide your divorce financial planning (sponsored):
http://divorcesavvy.com/

Qualified Domestic Relations Order (QDRO) - Basic Information and FAQ
https://www.dol.gov/agencies/ebsa/about-ebsa/our-activities/resource-center/faqs/qdro-overview

Links to California forms regarding child support and other financial issues

Child support

California Courts information on child support, including link to a California Guideline Child Support Calculator
http://www.courts.ca.gov/selfhelp-support.htm

Department of Child Support Services
http://www.ca.gov/Agencies/Child-Support-Services-Department-of/Agency-Services/Apply-for-Child-Support

Child Support forms can be found at the following link
http://www.courts.ca.gov/1199.htm, including a stipulation and order
http://www.courts.ca.gov/documents/fl350.pdf

Spousal support

Information on Spousal/Partner Support and forms
http://www.courts.ca.gov/1038.htm

Income and Expense Declaration form
http://www.courts.ca.gov/documents/fl150.pdf

PowerPoint on how to complete an Income and Expense Declaration:
http://www.occourts.org/self-help/resources/oc-courts/Income-Expense-Declaration.pptx

Budgeting and property division

Information on property division and forms
http://www.courts.ca.gov/1039.htm

Declaration of Disclosure form
http://www.courts.ca.gov/documents/fl140.pdf

Schedule of Assets and Debts form
http://www.courts.ca.gov/documents/fl142.pdf

Declaration Regarding Service of Declaration of Disclosure form
http://www.courts.ca.gov/documents/fl141.pdf

Judgment Checklist - Dissolution/Legal Separation
http://www.courts.ca.gov/documents/fl182.pdf

Pensions and retirement plans

General information:
http://www.qdrodesk.com/qdro/The-QDRO-and-the-Divorce-Decree-Settlement-164.shtml

Social Security – Information for divorcing spouses

Benefits planner:
https://www.ssa.gov/planners/index.html

Retirement estimator:
https://www.ssa.gov/retire/estimator.html

Benefits as a spouse:
https://www.ssa.gov/planners/retire/applying6.html

Internal Revenue Service – Pension, IRA and retirement information

Types of retirement plans:
https://www.irs.gov/Retirement-Plans/Plan-Sponsor/Types-of-Retirement-Plans-1

Retirement Plan FAQ:
https://www.irs.gov/Retirement-Plans/Retirement-Plans-Frequently-Asked-Questions-FAQs-1

IRA accounts:
https://www.irs.gov/Retirement-Plans/Individual-Retirement-Arrangements-(IRAs)-1

Distributions from IRA:
https://www.irs.gov/publications/p590b/index.html

Internal Revenue Service – Tax issues

IRS Publication 504, Divorced or Separated Individuals
https://www.irs.gov/pub/irs-pdf/p504.pdf.

Qualified Domestic Relations Order (QDRO)

Basic information and FAQ
https://www.dol.gov/sites/default/files/ebsa/about-ebsa/our-activities/resource-center/faqs/qdro-overview.pdf

BOOKS AND ARTICLES ON DIVORCE

There are many helpful books and aricles for people considering or working through a divorce. These are a limited selection we believe provide helpful information with a balanced approach that will help you think for yourself and make good, practical decisions.

Helpful advice from the other side of divorce:
Crazy Time: Surviving Divorce and Building a New Life by Abigail Trafford

Guide to help think through your divorce:
A Comparison of Dispute Resolution Methods Available in Family Law Matters by Mark Baer
https://www.markbaeresq.com/documents/Baer-Chapter.pdf
The Divorce Organizer & Planner by Brette Semb

Parenting advice:
Putting Children First: Proven Parenting Strategies for Helping Children Thrive Through Divorce by JoAnne Pedro-Carroll

The Co-Parents' Handbook: Raising Well-Adjusted, Resilient, and Resourceful Kids in a Two-Home Family by Karen Bonnell and Kristin Little

The Co-Parenting Survival Guide: Letting Go of Conflict After a Difficult Divorce by Elizabeth Thayer Ph.D

Basic divorce guide and information
http://www.divorcesupport.com/divorce/Divorce-eBooks-1762.html

Divorce, Simply Stated: How to Achieve More, Worry Less and Save Money in Your Divorce" by Larry Sarezky

How to manage a cooperative divorce process
Between Love and Hate: A Guide to Civilized Divorce by Lois Gold

Putting Kids First in Divorce: How to Reduce Conflict, Preserve Relationships and Protect Children During and After Divorce": by Various Authors

Managing conflict after divorce:
The Co-Parenting Survival Guide: Letting Go of Conflict After a Difficult Divorce by Elizabeth Thayer Ph.D.

Classic book about joint parenting:
Mom's House, Dad's House: Making two homes for your child by Isolina Ricci Ph.D.

Helpful advice in a humorous approach:
How to Avoid the Divorce From Hell: (and dance together at your daughter's wedding) by M. Sue Talia

Helpful Books on Divorce
Divorce Mediation in California by Julie Gentili Armbrust

Mom's House Dad's House by Isolina Ricci, Ph.D

The Healthy Divorce, Keys to Ending Your Marriage While Preserving Your Emotional Well-Being by Lois Gold

Between Love and Hate, How to Resolve Conflict, Improve Communication and Avoid Costly Legal Battles by Lois Gold

"Divorce, Simply Stated: How to Achieve More, Worry Less and Save Money in Your Divorce" by Larry Sarezky

A FINAL WORD

We hope this book has provided useful information and helpful suggestions for traveling the journey of separation and divorce. Our objective was to offer some tools to help you make smart and practical decisions about your future life, parenting your children and your finances.

Of course, no book can make the decisions for you. This is up to you. We can provide some guidance, but in the end, you know best what is right for you and for your family.

The effects of separation or divorce do not stop on the day you sign your agreement, especially if you have children. The finances and asset division, debt responsibility and plan for parenting your children will affect your life for many years. And, that's why we believe it is so important for you to make decisions that are good for you and your family. That's why we believe so strongly in you and your ability to be smart and capable. That's why we believe you should be in charge of these decisions.

We want to offer a few final hints and recommendations that will allow you to make the best of a difficult situation, to have a good and happy future, to raise strong and lively children.

First, recognize the decision to separate and divorce is only the beginning for you. It's important to acknowledge the phases of grief (see page 2) and to realize you will face a variety of challenges along the way.

Second, take each step seriously and with a clear purpose. No one goes through divorce in the same way, in the same time period, and with the same emotions. You are unique. Don't compare your experience with anyone else's.

Third, maintain your balance—it's not easy—between what you need to do in the moment (grocery shopping, making lunches, driving the kids to school, going to work) and what you need to do for the future (make a plan for your children, work out finances).

Fourth, there is tremendous pressure to move forward, to put the past in the past and start again. You want to end the pain, stop feeling anxious or bitter, begin to feel "like yourself" again. The best way forward is to make a solid and workable agreement with your spouse. Be patient, stay focused on your goals, be courageous and if necessary, be fierce.

Fifth, make a good agreement. The best test of whether an agreement is fair and reasonable is to ask: "Will it really work?" For most people going through divorce, this means talking with your spouse—whether that happens over the "kitchen table," with a mediator or collaborative lawyer. If your spouse is not willing to work with you, then find a capable attorney to help you obtain a fair and practical settlement.

Sixth, make the agreement work. Yes, it's hard work to negotiate and make decisions; it's not always easy to deal with your spouse about finances or your children. Your best path to a happy life is to make sure the road ahead is free of obstacles. Find ways to work with your spouse, when possible, and that will ease your burden.

We would never suggest this is a simple or easy path. There will be moments when it seems impossible to agree on anything with your spouse. There will be times when you are overwhelmed with the difficulty of parenting your children or paying your bills. At some points, you will feel lost, think it's all hopeless. All this is real and understandable. Everyone who goes though a divorce has these thoughts, fears and feelings. We tell you this because you aren't crazy. Yet, divorce can make you feel crazy sometimes. That's real. But it's not forever.

You have the chance to complete this journey with dignity and self-respect. No one can take that from you. It might get messy. It might not be easy. But with the information and tools in this book, you have the best chance of ending up with a solid, workable and fair agreement and the best chance for a happy future.

Made in United States
Orlando, FL
01 February 2022

14287754R00106